In Fellowship

A book of
remembrance for
Brenda Walker

We acknowledge the First Nations Peoples of the lands on which we live and work, tell stories and remember.

Cover art: *Lake* by David Bailey, oil on canvas, 92.0 cm × 61.0 cm. Collection of the Estate of Brenda Walker.

This volume was compiled by Georgia Richter, with assistance from Anne-Louise Willoughby and Naama Grey-Smith, December 2024.

Cover design by Carolyn Brown, tendeersigh.com.au.

For all who loved Brenda,
and whose lives she touched.

Contributors

Alex Ruskulis – Rose bed (a poem for Brenda, 2013)

Where elegant blooms met the eye
Only stubs remain
Branches cut by a gardener's hand
Those reds, those pinks, those purples
That enchanted and entranced are no more
Their enraptuous spell in summer and autumn at last overcome by winter

A few petals still veil the ground
A reminder of happy times past
Laughter, joy, the dreams of the future seem all lost now
A sombre time
A time of reflection, thought, solitude
Thoughts turn to life, its meaning, its purpose

Yet an unobtrusive bud manifests
A beat of life
An unshakeable spirit that resists the domination of winter
Its purpose to the observer is yet obscure
But on the morrow it will be larger, stronger, more resolute
It contains an unrelenting desire of future
No obstacle, no challenge will deter its purpose
And yet again the garden will be filled with those same reds, pinks, purples

—

Alex Ruskulis met Brenda Walker in 2013 and married her in 2015.

Delia Falconer – Vale Brenda Walker, 1957–2024

I first met Brenda Walker in 1995 at Varuna, The National Writers' House in Katoomba, where she was working on her third novel and I was working on my first. The yellow house above the cliffs had been the author Eleanor Dark's home. Her annotated research books were still on the shelves and her son's gilded baby shoes on the mantel.

Within days, we had struck up a deep and sustaining friendship. In an early draft of Brenda's novel *Poe's Cat* (1999), I was the writer who climbed to the widows' walk to watch the clouds. But Brenda was fearless in making swift cuts as she arranged strands of calm unspooling prose. In the final version, the too-close cousins Thea and Finn meet in a house that is still modelled on Varuna, with its long rhododendron-lined driveway, but it has become a dead relative's half-abandoned home.

Across her five-book oeuvre, which included the novel *The Wing of Night* (2005) and the memoir *Reading by Moonlight: How Books Saved a Life* (2010), Brenda's writing and speaking voices were strikingly alike: tranquil, sharply observant, buoyed by a light sense of wonder.

An assiduous journal keeper, she would often take details of the environments in which she had lived – the northern rivers of New South Wales, Sydney's inner east, Perth – and tip them into heightened patterns of human light and shade. Over the years

I would look forward to hearing her voice on the phone from Perth, or in texts or emails, often recounting a dream or funny detail that she thought would give me pleasure. During a terrible time in my life she would keep me alive with her steadying calls, bringing firmness and courage to the act of navigating with me through my loss.

When the Soviet literary critic Viktor Shklovsky fell in love with Elsa Triolet while he was in hiding in Berlin, she would accept his daily letters only on the condition that they never mention his romantic feelings. Yet Shklovsky's lively dispatches to Triolet about writing, art, and German and Russian life, still crackled with the forbidden emotion, all the stronger for its suppression. Shklovsky's novel *Zoo, or Letters Not About Love,* published in 1923, was a touchstone book for Brenda, who delighted in its tension between lovesickness and restraint, its transformation of exile and rupture.

But it was Samuel Beckett, whom she discovered at nineteen, who was her lodestone, and key to the dance of lush and strict in her own writing. Reading the Irish writer's minimalist prose aloud, she wrote, allowed one to slip into a calm state that had nothing to do with resignation. She admired Beckett for his 'great capacity to steady himself, to live with simplicity and steadiness whatever the circumstances. Nothing can be achieved otherwise'.

~

Brenda Walker was born in Grafton in 1957, the younger sister of two brothers. The family's house on the river had a resident poltergeist, which, as she recorded in fictional form in the story 'Mrs Holland', she would sometimes hear her father gently chiding. The enduring motifs of her writing life were laid down in this lush riverine environment.

In a primal scene that Walker memorialised in different texts, her father dived in deep floodwaters to free the tow rope of the boat that would take the family to safety. Dreams of unstable water, she wrote in *Reading by Moonlight*, would recur throughout her life.

Brenda's childhood was also marked by stories of young rural men lost on the battlefields of two world wars and the tough women who waited for them. Among the living ghosts who did return was Walker's paternal grandfather, his face badly maimed by shrapnel. When she was fourteen, she moved with her mother to Armidale. The mummified head of an Egyptian girl resided in a wooden box in the school library. It would appear often in her writing. So too would characters living in coastal cities, who felt the pull of rural hinterlands where deep practicality coexisted with hidden damage.

After completing her undergraduate degree in Armidale, and her PhD on Beckett's fiction at Australian National University in Canberra, Walker moved to Perth in 1984 to take up a lectureship at the University of Western Australia; she would rise to the position of Winthrop Chair of English Literature and

Cultural Studies, the first female professor in the history of the department.

In 1990, she won the TAG Hungerford Award for a work in manuscript and her novel *Crush* (1991) was published by Fremantle Arts Centre Press. An experimental crime novel about storytelling and fathers told in a springy, condensed prose, it drew lightly on her academic work on writing and gender.

For fellow writer Deborah Robertson, her forensic but tender writing brought a fresh eye to the city. 'Her mordant wit, the lash of her intellect, her felt understanding of perversity and corruption and the unseen – they all worked to penetrate a city that was otherwise hard to see and understand – all that blinding light, erasure of memory, bullying wealth.'

Now part of an astonishing generation of young Western Australian women writing lyrical, ambitious fiction, Walker published *One More River* (1993). In the novel, her unconventional narrator Faith Bright goes on the run with her young bloke from her river-island home in northern New South Wales to Sydney's gritty Kings Cross, familiar territory to Walker, who visited her musician brother there often in the 1980s. The novel was adapted for screen and the script went through various stages of development but the film remains unmade.

Poe's Cat, published in 1999, balanced the contemporary story of Australian cousins Thea and Finn against Edgar Allan Poe's marriage to his thirteen-year-old cousin Virginia Clemm. The novel continued Walker's exploration of gender and storytelling as Thea appropriated characters from the novelist's disturbing oeuvre into tender stories that aimed to 'put the love back into Poe'.

Based on research Walker undertook as a visiting fellow at Stanford and Virginia universities, the novel also established an enduring North American connection. NYU-based critic Nicholas Birns described Walker as one of the three best prose stylists in Australia. *Poe's Cat* was shortlisted for the Western Australian, Victorian and New South Wales Premier's literary awards.

The Wing of Night drew on childhood stories of war-damaged men and women, though Brenda was also thinking of the second Gulf War. The novel shifts obliquely between the horrors of horseback warfare for the Australian Light Horse men and animals on the Middle Eastern desert battlefields of World War I and the women on Western Australian farms waiting for them. It earned an Asher Award for a novel with an anti-war theme for its invocation of the ongoing harms of global violence. Its surefootedness belied its difficult completion during Walker's treatment for breast cancer.

Brenda would write about the books that sustained her during the treatment and recovery from this breast cancer in her memoir *Reading by Moonlight*. Looping with a clarified intelligence through a lifetime of reading and living, it was intended for other readers who might need to find the company of the right book in times of crisis. She loved novels, she wrote, for their sense of human largeness – 'where dream and memory, impulse, unforeseeable events and helpless longing are part of otherwise rational lives'. The book brought her new readers and won the Nita B Kibble and Victorian Premier's literary awards.

'I thought this may be my last book but I seem to have survived,' Walker told an interviewer,[1] 'and the book marks a point of division in my life and work. I was very interested in the Australian response to war, in Australian rural life, and in the historical novel. I'm still interested in these things, but the projects I am working on are more contemporary and autobiographical or stimulated by my immediate circumstances. My memoir helped me to see the value of that.'

❧

Walker published her creative work while sustaining a demanding academic career, in which she also achieved significant academic publications, including editing books on gender and poetry[2] and the writing of Elizabeth Jolley.[3] She also edited and contributed

---

1 'KR Conversations', *Kenyon Review*, kenyonreview.org/conversation/brenda-walker, 17 April 2017.

2 *Poetry and gender: statements and essays in Australian women's poetry and poetics*, edited by David Brooks and Brenda Walker (UQP, 1989).

3 *Elizabeth Jolley: New Critical Essays*, edited by Delys Bird and Brenda Walker, (Angus & Robertson, 1991).

to the anthology *Risks*,[4] which drew together short fiction by major authors of the 1990s.

She is remembered as an inspirational teacher and supervisor of PhD Research, with many published authors stating that they would not have begun their careers or found the courage to publish without her.

Former colleague, Yasmin Haskell, UNESCO Chair in Intercultural and Interreligious Relations at Monash University, remembers Brenda as an '"*esprit de finesse*", whose mind and conversation bubbled with curiosity about literature and art from Ireland to Italy, Russia to Japan. She cherished her friendships with colleagues from Classics, Italian, History, Fine Arts and Philosophy.'

Walker's influence in building Australian writing with knowledge, skill and kindness extended beyond her state. In addition to her work as a mentor for Varuna, she was a member of the Australia Council's Literature Board from 2012 to 2014 and chair of the judging panel of the national Stella Prize for women's writing from 2016 to 2017.

In the days since her death, I have heard from many writers who received generous letters of encouragement, unbidden, in a spirit of solidarity. One recipient described being in the same room as her at the many festivals to which she was invited, in Ubud (Bali), Cheltenham (UK) and Australia, as 'magical'.

---

4 *Risks*, edited by Brenda Walker (Fremantle Arts Centre Press, 1996).

Yet Brenda's readers may be unaware of the significant body of short work that she produced before and after her retirement as emeritus professor.

These stories and essays – which explore key preoccupations of risk, motherhood, and the steadying forces of family and music – appeared in one-off Australian collections like Carmel Bird's *Daughters and Fathers*[5] and international literary journals. The story 'The Houses that are Left Behind'[6] in the journal *Kenyon Review*, won a prestigious O Henry Prize.[7]

I had the joy of commissioning work from Brenda twice for *Best Australian Stories*. 'Big Animals', about a mother and recovering daughter visiting Ubud, with its giant funerary animals and grim elephant shows, remains a personal favourite.[8] Our mothers, she wrote, are our first big animals. Brenda's joy in being a mother to her son Tom shone from many of these short works. 'In the night the baby and I turn about each other like the planets,' she recorded in one essay, 'as we shift from one breast to the other.'

In her last published works, two essays for the *Times Literary Supplement*,[9] Walker enlisted her beloved Beckett to think about

---

5 *Daughters and Fathers*, edited by Carmel Bird (UQP, 1997).

6 'The Stories that are Left Behind', *Kenyon Review*, New Series, Vol. 39, No. 2 (Mar/Apr 2017), pp. 72–80, jstor.org/stable/26451105.

7 'The Houses that are Left Behind', Brenda Walker, O Henry Prize Stories, brendawalker.com/o-henry-interview.

8 *The Best Australian Stories 2008*, edited by Delia Falconer (Black Inc., 2008).

9 'The constant noise of the earth: On breathing, Samuel Beckett, and Lenin's deathbed' and 'Nothing to be done: On Beckett and Australian bushfires' by Brenda Walker, the-tls.co.uk/authors/brenda-walker.

accelerating climate change and the future of the planet. The essays loop out across the dried-out gardens of once-lush Armidale, literature, the violence of colonial settlement, and Brenda's desk in her Perth apartment with its view of the Swan River.

The world comes to us through sound, she wrote from her quiet city, cut off from the rest of the world by the pandemic. Like Beckett's Molloy, she hoped she might be able to hear 'the far unchanging noise the earth makes'.

This acute attunement to sound, in the form of music, was another gift from her 'large steady family' in the east and another deep wellspring of her craft. The piano that echoed through the timber hallways of her childhood often made its way into her fiction, especially the arabesques, with its counterpoint and rapidly changing harmonies.

Daily work at the piano in the apartment near her beloved Kings Park, where she was settled happily with her husband Alex, was a joy. 'Yesterday my exacting teacher said, "You are in full control of this piano!"' she reported in August. 'And I WAS.'

It is as unthinkable that there will be no more work of Brenda's to read as it is that I can never speak with her again. A new novel, recently begun, was to be set in northern New South Wales and she was working on its separate pieces, in microcosm. We would meet again to write together soon. Perhaps in Rome, she messaged.

Keep in mind: streets lined with fruiting mandarins. An old man with a cat in a harness on a bus stop bench taking a little bottle of water from his backpack and a tin and pouring the cat a sip of water. These things are more precious than the Sistine Chapel.

—

Delia Falconer is the author of four books: *The Service of Clouds*, *The Lost Thoughts of Soldiers*, *Sydney* and *Signs and Wonders*.

This piece first appeared in theconversation.com/remembering-brenda-walker-245840, 16 December 2024.

Tony Hughes-d'Aeth & Kieran Dolin – Emerita Professor Brenda Walker (1957–2024)

The University of Western Australia mourns the passing on 10 December of Emerita Professor Brenda Walker at the age of sixty-seven. Brenda moved to UWA in 1984 to commence work as a lecturer in the Department of English. She retired in 2016 after a distinguished career that took her to the top of her profession. Brenda is remembered as a gifted teacher, scholar and creative writer. Her literary career ran in parallel to her work in the academy. Indeed, Brenda was one of the founders – with Dennis Haskell, Van Ikin and Stephen Chinna – of the creative writing program at UWA in the 1990s. Brenda led this program for many years, developing its methodology and nurturing generations of students. Her collection *The Writer's Reader* (2002) was a seminal textbook for creative writing as a university discipline in Australia and was the first such book to draw largely on contributions from contemporary Australian writers. That the creative writing program continues to flourish at UWA is one of Brenda's lasting legacies.

When creative writing doctorates were approved at UWA, Brenda became a mentor to the many Western Australian writers that came through that degree. Her national reputation as a writer and critic also attracted aspiring interstate writers to the UWA program. Her students valued her unerring eye for craft, her passion for literary prose and her often wicked sense of humour. Brenda was a valued colleague and leader in the discipline of English and Literary Studies. She led the discipline from 2013 to 2015.

Brenda's stature among students drew on her prize-winning books of fiction and memoir. Her novel, *Crush* (1991), won the TAG Hungerford Award for a first work of fiction. *One More River* (1993) was shortlisted for the WA Premier's Book Awards. A third novel, *Poe's Cat*, drew national acclaim, being shortlisted in the New South Wales and Victorian, as well as the Western Australian premier's awards. *The Wing of Night* (2005) won three awards, including the Nita B Kibble Literary Award for the best book by an established woman writer, and was shortlisted for the Miles Franklin Literary Award. Her next book was the memoir, *Reading by Moonlight: How Books Saved a Life* (2010), a reflection on her experience of cancer and the role played by reading during her treatment and recovery. It won the Victorian Premier's Award for Non-Fiction and a second Nita B Kibble Literary Award. Her short story, 'The Houses That Are Left Behind' (2017), was selected for The O Henry Prize Stories anthology in the US.

As a critic and scholar, Brenda made significant contributions to feminist criticism, Australian literature and creative writing studies. With David Brooks she edited *Poetry and Gender: Statements and Essays in Australian Women's Poetry and Poetics* (1989). With Delys Bird she edited *Elizabeth Jolley: New Critical Essays* (1991), and co-wrote the introduction to *Killing Women: Rewriting Detective Fiction* (1993). She presented the 2011

Herbert Blaiklock Memorial Lecture at the University of Sydney, on the topic 'Alex Miller and Leo Tolstoy: Australian Storytelling in a European Tradition'.

After her retirement, Brenda remained connected to the University and to creative writing in Western Australia, continuing to supervise creative writing students with her trademark generosity of spirit. She was a regular reviewer for *Australian Book Review* and was a widely admired senior figure in the Australian literary community. Her loss is deeply felt throughout the country. Brenda Walker was an outstanding servant of UWA and has left an enduring mark in this academy and beyond.

—

Tony Hughes-d'Aeth is Chair of Australian Literature and **Kieran Dolin** is Senior Honorary Research Fellow in the School of Humanities at the University of Western Australia.

This piece first appeared in uwa.edu.au/news/article/2024/december/vale-brenda-walker, 19 December 2024.

Georgia Richter – Vale Brenda Walker (1957–2024)

> *... make an honest platform of story in your mind, like a raft, using the sound timber of everything you've loved and read. As with any raft, it may sometimes feel unsteady; it may falter under the weight it must carry, and, over time, it will need repair. It may not withstand the sea for all eternity but nor does it need to – it needs to last a lifespan, nothing more.*
>
> – from *Reading by Moonlight*

It is with profound sadness that I and my colleagues at Fremantle Press acknowledge the untimely and sudden death of Brenda Walker, esteemed writer, Winthrop Professor of English and Cultural Studies at the University of Western Australia, past Stella Prize chair, and friend and mentor to many – a gentle, generous, considerate person and a writer of immense talent and deep insight.

In 2020, Brenda was one of the three external judges of the City of Fremantle Hungerford Award, on the anniversary of thirty years since she herself won the inaugural Hungerford with her brilliant first novel, *Crush* (1991). Of her Hungerford win, Brenda said, '*There is no better way for a Western Australian writer to make the transition from solitary work to the literary community and the world of readers.*' *Crush* marked the beginning of a superlative writing career that saw Brenda become adored and admired nationally and beyond. *One More River* followed (Fremantle

Press, 1993), then *Poe's Cat* (1999), *The Wing of Night* (2005) and her memoir *Reading by Moonlight: How Books Saved a Life* (2010).

Brenda was awarded many times for her writing – winning the Nita B Kibble Literary Award twice, a Victorian Premier's Literary Award, the Asher Literary Award and the Waverley Library Award for Literature, and the O Henry Prize in the US, as well as numerous shortlistings in state and national awards, including the Miles Franklin Literary Award.

My own life first intersected with Brenda's via her writing. When I flew home from Perth to Melbourne the very first time, I gave my mother a copy of *Crush*, because I wanted to share with her its edgy, elegant, good-humoured West Australianness – an urbane thriller like no other I'd read before.

Decades on, in 2010, I gave my mother *Reading by Moonlight*, inscribed by Brenda with the words *For Kay, in fellowship* – a gift between two readers who both knew cancer and who knew the solace to be found in books in the middle of the dark night. I know that Brenda must have touched thousands of lives in the same way through her writing.

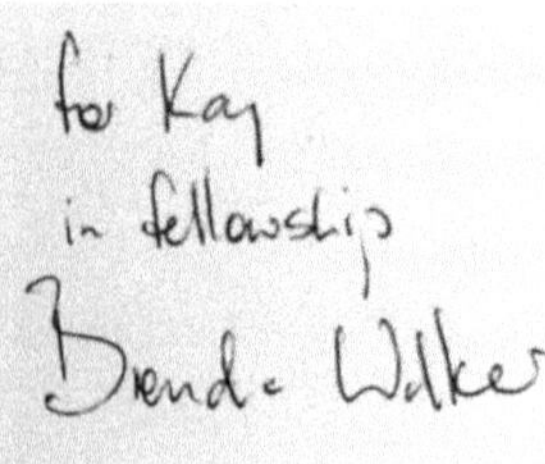

When I arrived in Perth in the summer of 1993, I had to decide whether I would enrol in the masters program at Curtin University or join the inaugural Master of Creative Writing program at UWA. My Melbourne University honours supervisor, Kerryn Goldsworthy, had already reached out to her friend Brenda Walker at UWA (Kerryn phoned Brenda to ask her to look out for me while I sat with her in her office on campus). And so Brenda was the person who first met me on the UWA campus – willowy, ethereal, kindly smiling beneath an enormous sunhat. Almost immediately, she said, 'Let me show you a few of the places that I love.' And so we drove in her car together, and I gazed out at the blue Derbarl Yerrigan (known to me in those days as the Swan River) and through Kings Park with its dense warm smell of eucalyptus.

As we talked, it began to dawn on me with a slow kind of wonder that Brenda was speaking to me as if I was already a colleague of hers. In that exact moment, I moved from undergrad to postgrad, from a girl finding her way to an adult whose opinions were sought and valued. We were writers together – two women talking who both loved language, and stories and words. I was a writer! I had arrived!

It was this car ride with Brenda that made me choose UWA, where I became the first of two masters students in a new creative writing program run by Brenda and her colleagues Dennis Haskell and Van Ikin. And it was this warm, easy gesture of hers that instilled in me the sense that the Western Australian writing community was collegiate, generous, inclusive and welcoming.

I never forgot that gift of levelling Brenda had bestowed upon me. I thought of it when I met new students and – later, as publisher – new authors, and I was mindful to follow her example that every new Western Australian writer is worth nurturing, and that we wordsmiths are fundamentally bound by our love of the craft, no matter where on the path of experience we may be. When I became a tutor in creative writing, I drew on and urged students to read Brenda's helpful and informative *The Writer's Reader: A Guide to Writing Fiction and Poetry* (2002).

I spoke to Brenda often over the years as her writing career flourished and mine morphed into one of editing and publishing. We became colleagues in a different way. I can't count the number of times Brenda said to me, 'Let me know how I can support the press' – and so she provided statements of support for Fremantle Press, and read the manuscripts of new authors to provide cover quotes for their books and, of course, accepted the invitation to judge the 2020 City of Fremantle Hungerford Award with Richard Rossiter and Sisonke Msimang. This was a monumental undertaking for which she was perfectly suited as a discerning wordsmith, a clever and passionate reader and an identifier of writing talent in others.

Many of our authors have told me across time that Brenda encouraged them in their writing or supervised their theses that we were now publishing, and how she was a friend, champion, exacting practitioner, canny therapist and gentle guide all at once. I had already learned, during my own masters, that Brenda did not ask for vulnerability without giving it in return – and that better, more genuine writing would always be the result.

Only once, recently, did Brenda refuse an invitation, and that was to come to the 2024 Hungerford ceremony to celebrate with alumni and to meet the new winner. She sent warm wishes and regrets, but was looking forward to a trip to Oslo with her beloved husband, Alex. This email exchange is my final correspondence with her and it is easier to think of her somewhere out in the world, filtering its richness and its beauty through her private wordscape, than that she should not be here anymore.

I know that in the Fremantle Press family – both in-house and amongst our authors and collaborators – we who knew and loved her are mourning her passing. If there is supposed to be a pattern or a meaning in anything, it has felt terribly disrupted and broken this week. Brenda's death makes no sense, and it reminds us that life is precious, too brief, and sometimes very unfair.

So it is that I am left thinking of all those accrued moments of warmth and generosity from one of the most lovely human beings I have ever known – the sum of many beautiful parts it is much too soon to be totalling.

Vale, Brenda. Thank you for all you did for us. The reach of your good deeds and beautiful words will continue far beyond a lifespan that has ended much too soon.

—

Georgia Richter is Publisher of Fiction, Narrative Non-Fiction and Poetry at Fremantle Press.

This piece first appeared in fremantlepress.com.au/2024/12/13/vale-brenda-walker-1957-to-2024, 13 December 2024.

Christine Balint – Vale Brenda Walker

Brenda Walker appeared in my life at significant moments. I first met her during a mentorship program at Varuna in 1998. I was a young student and had just completed honours in English at the University of Melbourne. I was at a crossroads: I wanted to keep writing and studying but was not sure where this would lead. For a week, Brenda mentored a group of us, which also included Charlotte Wood, Gerry Turcotte and Juliana Ryan. The reverberations of this week were felt by all of us for years to come. What I remember about this time, was Brenda's warmth and care. Her feedback on my work was insightful and always encouraging. Alongside these individual sessions, she counselled us on the writing life. There was great openness and laughter. Brenda and I kept in touch for a while; she read and endorsed the final draft of my novel, *The Salt Letters*, which emerged from this mentoring. Her examiner's report of my PhD in 2004 was thoughtful and generous, and I believe, helped me to secure an academic position at La Trobe University almost twenty years later. There is a whole generation of us – Australian writers and academics – who connected with each other and developed our careers under her gentle guidance and support.

—

Dr Christine Balint is the author of three novels and the mother of two children. She is a lecturer in English and Creative Writing at La Trobe University.

Carmel Bird – Remembering Brenda

In 1997, when recalling her memory of her father's coffin, Brenda wrote: 'He isn't in it. He's still moving around.'

With Brenda's own cruel and violent death, her graceful and elegant spirit has leapt into the hearts and minds of all who knew her, loved, read her. I hear her soft melodious speech, her low and lyrical laughter, the precision of her words. I see her tall balletic walk, her broad and welcoming smile, the steady kindly look with which she gently fixed her audience. The sophistication. The generosity. The charm. The beautiful smile. The tiny insects of her handwriting.

I heard the brutal news of her accident, and quite soon I placed in front of me her books – tangible objects inhabited by Brenda, pages that were her rich gift to her readers. I opened the anthology *Daughters and Fathers* in which her essay on her father heads the collection, and there I found this photo, Brenda in 1997, in all her youthful glory.

I recalled how it was when I first saw this picture, and was struck by the image of her left hand, so relaxed it seems to melt as it dangles from her wrist. These fingers typed the novels and stories and essays. They played Brenda's piano. There is a watch, or bracelet on her wrist, and the sight of this reminded me of a necklace she once gave me.

I took out the necklace and stared at it – turned it over in my hands, meditating, I suppose – somehow trying to infuse my sorrow with the sight of it. A string of seventeen icy, minty green glass beads resembling boiled lollies. Flashing inside each heavy bead is a kind of silvery leaf that is laced with fine gold lines. There is a little world in there. Between the green beads are tiny black glass beads that look like jet. Long ago, those long, fine fingers held these beads, wrapped them in whispering tissue paper, and sent them across the country to me. I had never before sat and stared at them, lightly fingered them. Nor had I previously connected them with the green glass beads in the haunting little poem by Harold Monro, a favourite from childhood, 'Overheard on a Saltmarsh'. The nymph in the poem 'stole them out of the moon'. I imagine discussing all this with Brenda. She smiles. Like her father, she is 'still moving around'. With immense sadness, I remember Brenda.

—

Carmel Bird (carmelbird.com) is an Australian writer.

Delys Bird – In memory of Brenda Walker

It seems extraordinary to be able to say that it's forty years since a young, quite newly PhD'd, quite newly married and arrived in Perth, Brenda Walker came to see me at the English Department at UWA. Her mother, Shirley Walker, an academic and writer, had been a very dear if distant friend and colleague of mine for some years so we had a significant connection. Brenda was an aspiring academic (and writer though I didn't know that then) and we talked about what became her successful application for a position in UWA's large and flourishing English Department. She quickly established herself as an important and valued member of that department, and widely known and admired as a teacher and writer, critic and reviewer. Brenda and I collaborated in the early 1990s on a book of essays on Elizabeth Jolley's work and co-wrote an introduction to a collection of pieces by Australian women crime writers. All during the time her son Tom was born; she won the Hungerford Award for her unpublished manuscript of *Crush*; and she carried out the multifarious duties of academic life. Always responsive and impressively competent, Brenda was a witty and wise, and often tender, observer of life and its follies. Hard to believe that we won't bump into each other in the aisles of our local supermarket, as we sometimes did, when she would quickly tell me tales of her full and very happy life.

—

Delys Bird AM has been a teacher, critic, judge of literary awards and long-time co-editor of *Westerly Magazine*.

Nicholas Birns – Tribute to Brenda Walker

I first made contact with Brenda Walker in summer 1994, when I reviewed, in the US-based journal *Antipodes*, an anthology called *Reading from the Left* edited by Wendy Jenkins. I believe the rationale for this book was non–Western Australian writer picking a Western Australian writer; in this case, Sara Dowse picked Brenda Walker, whom she had known in Canberra. After Brenda saw my particular mention of her work in this review, we corresponded and then saw each other when she visited New York in February 1997, as she was working on *Poe's Cat*. We continued to see each other as she visited New York during the 1990s and 2000s, and in 2003 or so she visited my class on the historical novel at The New School. I also got to see her in Perth the one time so far I visited there in 2012.

Brenda was a warm, lively, invigorating person who was always cheering to see and always conveyed a positive, affirmative, and enthusiastic feeling. This was done, though, with great subtlety and discernment, as she approached every conversation with the care with which she certainly approached her writing. She was unfailingly positive about fellow Australian writers and, at a time when my portfolio as book review editor and then editor of *Antipodes* was to promote the entire Australian literary field, this sympathy towards a broad range of writers was heartening and exemplary for me.

Brenda was a caring and kind person who was always interested in what was going on in other people's lives. When I got married in 2017, she wrote me and my wife a very warm note, which was very sad to reread and light of her untimely and shocking passing. She was at a very strong point in her writing just now, and probably several more decades of creative achievement were taken from her as we lost her the same year that her mother passed away.

As important as her fiction and nonfiction oeuvre was, we should not forget the role she played as a teacher of writing. She approached teaching writing with an exquisite sense of delicacy and craft. When she talked about her teaching, it reminded me of an Italian Renaissance painter or composer, who took apprentices; that sense of concentration, of resolution, of tact. But unlike a model where the apprentices were expected to be just like the teacher, the students were encouraged to go their own direction and bring to fruition that which was most compelling within them.

Her first two novels, *Crush* and *One More River*, both had very striking and very different lead female characters, Anna Penn and Faith Bright. What I admired in those portraits is that they had every potential to become symbolic or to be just inscriptions of the author; but instead they remained vividly and spectacularly themselves, almost resisting the very literary style and panache in which they were enclosed.

In *Poe's Cat* she wrote a story that was essentially on two levels, one about Edgar Allan Poe's relationship with Virginia Clemm, the other about true cousins, living more or less in the present named Thea and Finn, who had an illicit romance as young people. Brenda told me that when she attempted to pitch this book to US agents and publishers, they said that there was no audience in the US for fiction written on two temporal levels, a response I found absurd, given that this was the late 1990s and AS Byatt's *Possession* was the literary sensation of the decade. But upon further reflection, upon rereading the novel more recently, I see that the book does not in fact, exist on two levels at all. There is a thematic and effective and tonal unity and the two levels of time are just illustrations of this unity. What seems to be a detachable frame is in fact an inextricable field.

The Wing of Night (written about splendidly by the Canadian critic Donna Coates) portrays Gallipoli, the most iconic episode in Australian history, from the point of view of two very different women. Again, I feel it was somewhat misdiagnosed as a historical novel – although it certainly has a historical setting it was published in the aftermath of the Iraq war and to me could as well have been about twenty-first-century warfare and the inextricable relation of trauma to warfare; that war never totally happens when it happens and certainly does not end when it ends, not for the soldiers who fought, not their loved ones and survivors. Walker's style in this novel is limpid, severe, with a kind of lapidary eloquence that makes us realise that the story is of literary consequence, but does not remind us every minute we are reading out that this is literature with a capital L.

Because of its distinctive topography and history, and its distance from other world centres of English, the international reception of the Australian novel has tended to privilege content. Brenda, conversely, thought about narrative in terms of form, style, and even more shape. Her writing was not precious, nor was overly filled with literary illusions or her own wide reading. It was simply deeply thought about and deeply felt and written with a sense of dedication and delight.

—

Nicholas Birns teaches at New York University and was recently the co-editor of the *Cambridge Companion to the Australian Novel.*

Peter Bishop – Varuna, The National Writers' House

When I became director of Varuna in 1994, Brenda was one of my first guests. Varuna was something new in the world, and I – with a background of culture and enthusiasm rather than experience – was thrilled with its possibilities. Brenda treasured my culture and enthusiasm – and was immensely generous in sharing her experience and providing tactful guidance. We did wonderful things in those early years, and Brenda was foundational to the community we created. She gave me very valuable advice in proposing the Residential Mentorship program – and she was the first mentor I engaged. And her first choice among the writers who submitted was Charlotte Wood. They truly were wonderful times, and Brenda was at the heart of them.

Brenda also greatly encouraged me in the role I was developing as a consultant/friend/tactful guide for writers. With no university degree I was at first a little diffident – but Brenda was a writer who valued my particular capacity for insight and companionship, and she nurtured me beautifully. I can't think of a writer to whom I owe more.

My Varuna years are long passed – but I'm shortly to launch a program that grows out of the community we created through those years: The Writer Conversation. I was so looking forward to the time when I would share The Writer Conversation with Brenda: she would have given me enthusiasm and wisdom in equal measure. I can't begin to describe the sadness I feel that she will not be one of my secret sources of strength – and that the community we will create will not have Brenda as an abiding benevolent presence. I can't bear it that Brenda – gracious, subtle, endlessly surprising Brenda – won't be with us. Though of course – all she has been for me is essential to who I am, so she will always be a presence – and a vital one – in all that I do. And for so many – she will be a generative presence, a permanent spring, a counsel for creativity. This is the saddest possible news, and I haven't begun to marshal my thoughts in the way Brenda deserves. That time will come – but for now – these grieving words …

—

Peter Bishop was the creative director at Varuna, The National Writers' House from 1994 to 2010.

Fiona Britton – Tribute to Brenda Walker

Brenda Walker was impossibly elegant, fiendishly smart and wickedly funny.

Of course, as I write that now, I imagine her taking a red pen to every one of those adverbs. But I will keep them in, because this is a time for superlatives.

It's hard to express the impact Brenda has had in my life. I was seventeen when I first sat in her undergraduate class. And I was in awe.

At fifty-one, I remain in awe of her intellect and skill as a writer, her generosity, her capacity for great kindness, and her fealty as a friend.

Brenda remained present, with unfailing encouragement and saintly patience, for every dubious step of my development as a writer over thirty years. She tolerated my awkward early short stories, full of undergraduate overshares. She shrugged off my failed attempt at honours. Then, after my return to writing following the birth of my second child, she endured my 'tortured poet' phase. Next came the PhD novel which has taken its rightful place in a dark bottom drawer. And lastly, when the publishing gods finally smiled, she cheered me on through the publication of my first novel in 2023.

She is mentioned in the acknowledgements of that novel for saying: 'But you're so funny in real life, Fiona. Why isn't that on the page?' Thank you, Brenda. If anyone ever laughs at one of my jokes, it's due to you.

Brenda knew my dad (David Britton, a playwright) and over the years had come to know of all the members of my family, through our conversations. I was always deeply touched by the care and curiosity Brenda showed about my siblings, in particular. In some ways, my conversations with Brenda were a sort of through-line, from my teenage to mid-life. I understand now that a relationship such as this comes along once in a lifetime. Over the course of thirty years, I developed a picture of Brenda's family life too.

I send you most heartfelt sympathies, Alex and Tom, from my family to yours.

~

'Living in Perth is like falling asleep in the snow,' Brenda once told me, with a laugh. This must have been on one of my return visits from Sydney, during my PhD.

That quip was on my mind the morning she died.

We were to catch up soon. She had offered to take me for a 'welcome home' lunch and I couldn't wait to tell her that, after withstanding Sydney's nerve-jangling pace for nearly thirty years, I was ready to surrender, at last, to the sleepy, enveloping West Australian calm.

I imagined how hard we would laugh at this, since Brenda had been privy to some of my most (ahem) rocknroll secrets and had come to know my taste for adventure. I imagined how nice it would be to exchange work with her again. To drink so much coffee and talk so hard I'd come away giddy from the mental exertion. And I imagined how rich my new Perth life would be, with Brenda in it in a more regular way, because this year Brenda had been more than a writing mentor and friend to me. As I'd faced the distress of marriage breakdown over the last twelve months, Brenda had been a steadfast guide.

'Sleep, swim, recover, write,' she'd told me. These became words to live by.

As I write this now, I have a crystal-clear picture of Brenda Walker in my mind. We are at our last meeting, at the Holiday Inn in Potts Point, Sydney, over breakfast. I'm in a post-publication party phase so I turn up hungover and shabby, and I hoover up the scrambled eggs. It's not my finest hour, to say the least. She, on the other hand, is poised and calm and looks fantastic in a chic denim jumpsuit. She has just read my first novel in a single sitting and I'm ever so proud. I leave elated. My cup is full, and I remember another fabulous Brenda quip, delivered with a laugh: 'As writers, our wallets grow thin, but our souls grow fat and sleek.'

And today, I remember the words that concluded almost every exchange between Brenda and I about my writing. She always used the same sign off, offered the same encouraging push.

'Keep going,' she would say.

Keep going.

—

Fiona Britton splits her time between Perth and Sydney. She lives and writes on Bidjigal and Whadjuk Noongar land.

Wenona Byrne – Tribute from Creative Australia

Brenda Walker was a brilliant writer, editor, professor, and supporter of Australian literature who will be fondly remembered at Creative Australia (formerly the Australia Council for the Arts) and beyond as someone who made a telling difference, inspiring and educating future writers, and always acting with exceptional grace and integrity.

—

Wenona Byrne is Head of Literature at Creative Australia.

This first appeared in creative.gov.au/news/media-releases/vale-professor-brenda-walker, 13 December 2024.

Marion May Campbell – Brenda Walker: a tribute

The devastating news of Brenda's death brings with it a sense of excruciating loss to writing, as it does to literary scholarship. Her brilliance is manifest across the genres: whether short fiction, novella, novel, memoir, scholarly article, or PhD examination report. Her early doctoral engagement with Samuel Beckett might account in part for the decanted economy of her writing. Doubtless too, her researcher's ardour, her ethical vision, along with her urbane confidence, fed her stylish verve, her wry wit, her virtuosity in voicework, and her structural control – all of which marked her oeuvre as highly original and restlessly inventive.

What is striking to me, in returning to Brenda's first published novel, *Crush*, is her ability to mobilise a specifically Australian space, or chronotope, like that of the louvred veranda, as a leitmotif. The louvres mediate a singular, inevitably 'truncated', and 'corrugated' perception, albeit one driven by a passion to understand the passing stranger, the enigmatic other. Engaging with the capitalist corruption and seething violence just under the shonky surfaces of Perth's Northbridge in the late 1980s, the novel displays an acute awareness of the foundational violence of Invasion and the legacy of its suppression of sites of significance to the Whadjuk Noongar people. Concreted and trapped in travestied ponds, the swampland known as Boodjamooling, renamed by colonisers as Hyde Park, sees the murderous return of the repressed, which fuels this brilliant take on crime fiction. Brenda Walker is alive everywhere in her writing, whether fictional, autobiographical or scholarly – because it eschews ornamentation, enlisting with brilliant succinctness the complex lived texture of the moment and speaks, not only to the compassionate mind, but to all the senses of the embodied reader.

I am just one of hundreds of thousands who will be mourning this immeasurable loss, but who will keep finding consolation in the company of her beautiful books.

—

Marion May Campbell's most recent book is the poetry collection *languish* (Upswell, 2022).

Clare Carlin – (for) Brenda

Ironwood year
write something of her
water we can feel.
Can we verse an anchor
before the unrolling
trying words.
Witness her books
those shining houses
good-given.

Brenda was my creative writing honours supervisor in 2000. She was the first person to recognise me as a writer, and the source of many early writing opportunities. Thank you, Brenda.

—

Clare Carlin is a writer across forms and runs Ackland [Press].

Sophie Cunningham – Connection

I find it hard to remember Brenda in a formal way as I really am struggling to comprehend her death. I didn't see her often, but I treasured the times we did meet up (usually when I got to Perth) and the correspondence we shared between visits. I first met Brenda socially, through shared friends, in the early 1990s. In the decades since I had the opportunity to work with her several times. She was a member of the Literature Board when I was its chair, she was a judge of the Stella Prize when I was actively involved with that organisation, and I included a beautiful essay she wrote (everything Brenda wrote was beautiful) in an anthology that I edited in 2020, called *Fire, Flood, Plague*. These ongoing points of connection meant our friendship grew larger, and more solid. Brenda had such a talent for friendship and she was a loyal and supportive friend to so many of us in the literary community. Working with her also meant that I had the chance to see her glorious, big brain in action time and time again. She was clear, passionate, well-read, super smart, diplomatic but forthright. As well as a maker of literature, she was a great teacher of it. She talked often of her love for her husband, Alex, and her son. She adored her cats (who are extremely adorable). Her death is sudden, and it is devastating. I will miss her. So many of us will miss her. I take some solace in the knowledge she was much loved.

—

Sophie Cunningham is a writer of books, a teacher and Chair of the Australian Society of Authors.

Amanda Curtin – Falling silent

> *We can't stand the idea of our own voices falling silent finally, like a radio running down.*

So wrote Margaret Atwood in *The Blind Assassin.* And yet right now it's the opposite I'm having trouble with: the sudden snatching of life, the blunt instrument of random ill fortune, the senseless waste of something so fine.

That, I think, is why the death of Brenda Walker has been so profoundly shocking, so desperately sad, even to those who did not know her, or know her well.

I am one of the latter. I'd met Brenda, of course, spoken with her at various literary occasions, and had lunch with her once at the UWA Club, just to chat about books and bookish things. I remember that day, too, because it was not long before her wedding. A cliché, I know, but the word that springs to mind is entirely apt: she looked radiant.

I first came to know of Brenda in the early 1990s when she published her debut novel with what was then Fremantle Arts Centre Press. I had been working as a freelancer with the press since 1984, a period that served as my introduction to Western Australian literature, the intensely exciting, revelatory literature of my own place. I was employed to proofread the galleys of *Crush*, winner of the TAG Hungerford Award, and Brenda became one of the amazing women writers first published by FACP whom I would follow ever after, along with Gail Jones, Simone Lazaroo and Joan London.

This was the way I knew Brenda Walker best: through her writing. On my shelves are the novels *Crush*, *One More River*, *Poe's Cat, The Wing of Night*; and her moving memoir, *Reading by Moonlight: How Books Saved a Life*. *The Wing of Night* remains my favourite of her novels, and I think it was an influence on the direction into historical fiction that my own writing took, with its focus on women's lives and its validation of elemental matters often trivialised as domestic.

I join with the many in sending condolences to Brenda's family, friends and colleagues: I am so sorry for your devastating loss. And I am sorry for our collective loss, as felt by the writing and reading community. There were words yet to come, and Brenda Walker's voice should have been allowed to fall silent in its own time.

—

Amanda Curtin is the author of *Elemental, The Sinkings* (historical novels), *Inherited* (stories) and *Kathleen O'Connor of Paris* (narrative non-fiction).

Natalie Damjanovich-Napoleon – Reconstruction

loss loss the
accidental lover life

there's a photograph
doors a white dress

immense
white lilies

the light catches

the brightness

she

understood a great deal about suffering

drawn to the sea
shipwrecks

castaways islands

kinds of exile

a great longing for the sea water [s]he
cannot drink

stories travel

—

Natalie Damjanovich-Napoleon studied her BA at UWA with Brenda Walker. Her poetry is widely published in the US and Australia. She holds a PhD in creative writing from Edith Cowan University.

Words for this poem are borrowed from pp. 169–170 of Brenda Walker's *Reading by Moonlight: How books saved a life* (Penguin, 2010).

Stephen Dedman – In memoriam Brenda Walker

Firstly, a small confession: despite having worked with Brenda for many years, I haven't read very much of her work other than her novel *Poe's Cat* and some short stories, and the reasons I'll miss her – and I already miss her terribly – have little to do with the regret that we won't see any of the beautifully written fiction that she almost certainly would have given us in the next few decades. I don't know how much of my work she'd read, either; the genres we preferred to work in were very different, though we shared an interest in Poe. Our writing habits also differed, and Brenda often enthused about how prolific I was (oh, those were the days). I always had the feeling that she believed that the act of creative writing and finding your own voice was important regardless of whether you were a highly regarded literary writer or not, and she never made me feel embarrassed about primarily being a genre hack.

This mutual respect was only one of the things that made Brenda one of the best bosses I've ever had, and why I would always try to make myself available to teach the creative writing classes she organised (even while the university gradually reduced the number of tutoring hours and increased class sizes until they'd halved the former and doubled the latter). When the budget allowed, Brenda would try to give the tutors guest lecturer work and divide the exam marking between us, and she hired PhDs rather than save money by hiring candidates who could be paid less. This wasn't just for our benefit: it was so the students would have the benefit of being tutored by widely published writers with whom they could connect, whether the students were interested in writing poetry, literary fiction or non-fiction, fantasy or science fiction, or autobiography.

When Brenda announced that she was retiring, she was supportive of her tutors, including me, applying to take over her position, and she acted as my referee when I've applied for other teaching positions. And while I haven't seen her since then, we kept in touch by email and on social media, and at times when I was worried that my own life had been rather pointless, she would reassure me that I'd inspired at least some of my students and that that mattered.

I worked with Brenda while she survived cancer, and it seems horribly unfair that she's been taken away from us so suddenly in this way and that we have lost her voice – not just her literary voice, which I hope will remain in print forever, but the voice I heard in her office at meetings and when we saw each other in the corridors and discussed writing and publishing, the voice of a compassionate, considerate, inspiring teacher who cared about writing, and teaching, and her students. I will remember that voice, and I am very glad that I had the privilege of knowing her.

—

Dr Stephen Dedman taught creative writing at UWA from 2003 to 2016.

Jon Doust – A note to Brenda

Brenda, I was chairing a chat once, at the Sydney Writers Festival. The session was called: *Is there an ideal way? A right way? Brenda Walker and Mark Tredinnick talk about how they went about choosing the form for their memoirs* Reading by Moonlight *and* The Blue Plateau.

In my introduction I said of *Reading by Moonlight* that it took me on a journey through the past, the present, and the future, in one continuous stream, and sometimes I found myself weeping without knowing why, and I had to retrace my path, to find the words that built the waters.

It only took an hour of our time, but you and your words never left me.

You gave me your phone number. I have no memory of ever using it. Yet, from that first meeting on, whenever we met, our faces opened with a kind of joy, as though no time had passed, and that we had known each other for ever.

I think we had. I know we will.

—

Jon Doust lives and writes in Kinjarling, Albany.

Sara Dowse – From the beginning

I first knew Brenda when she and I, along with Dorothy Johnston, Margaret Barbalet and Elizabeth Tombs were in a writing group together. This was in Canberra in the early 1980s, if memory serves me right. None of us had published a book of fiction then – or any full-length literary work – but we were all intending to, and eventually did. Reading and critiquing one another's manuscripts was more valuable to me than anything I'd previously experienced in my apprenticeship, though Brenda, who was working on her doctorate on Beckett then, was the only scholar among us.

Shirley Hazzard's *The Transit of Venus* had a huge impact on us. I'm not sure that any of us would revere it now as we did at the time. Nor, as far as I can remember, did any of us know then of the specific circumstances of Hazzard's success. Our own lives were to be quite different from Hazzard's. Three of us already had young children; Brenda would have Tom after moving to Western Australia. He was just a baby when I stayed with her and her then-husband Tim in 1988 to take up a writer-in-residency at Curtin University. I remember them taking me to Northbridge, pleased to show me Perth's night life, which she would write about in *Crush*.

From the start, Brenda appreciated my writing. I think this was because both of our connections to music. She was especially supportive of my novel *Schemetime*, which drew in part on my growing up in Hollywood. I still treasure her commenting that the novel 'sang', and I've since learned that she made special mention of my work to at least one critic she came across. For my part, one of my most memorable images in literature is the opening passage of Brenda's *Wing of Night*.

Distance played its inevitable part. I can't recall if we wrote each other or, if we had, when the correspondence dwindled. I do remember my distress on learning she had breast cancer. But then there was the marvellous *Reading by Moonlight*, and her eventual recovery. We met for the last time in the late 1990s, in the parking lot of the Ainslie Rex, when Brenda was briefly in Canberra and I was about to leave for Canada, where I would spend five and a half years with my partner, Tony Taylor. She was delighted that I had found happiness with him, as was I on learning of hers with Alex. We never met, yet knowing what he gave her I can't even begin to measure the depth of his loss, or that of Tom's, or her brother Don's.

She died far too young and too suddenly. Like so many, I have been gutted by the news. Vale, then, to my friend, a gracious, funny, sweet-hearted woman who touched the hearts of so very many.

—

Sara Dowse is the author of six novels, the last of which is *As the Lonely Fly*, set in British Mandate Palestine.

Brooke Dunnell – What would Brenda cut?

Many have already articulated what a wonderful writer, teacher and person Brenda Walker was. She was all these things for me when I was lucky enough to have her supervise my PhD in Creative Writing. She helped me to think about my words deeply, craft them with care, and then seek out places where they might be shared. Her thoughtfulness and warmth were traits I tried to replicate when I began to tutor and mentor other writers. But she didn't just guide me in becoming a writer and a teacher – she had a hand in making me an adult.

I was twenty-one when I met Brenda. From high school I'd gone straight into an honours degree in English and Creative Writing, then moved on to postgraduate study just as the wave of the Great Recession was beginning to crest. I still lived at home, where I shared a twenty-year-old car with my brother and was on the verge of breaking up with my first boyfriend. I didn't know anything about anything. The first time I entered the UWA Arts Building, I saw a peacock halfway down a corridor and froze, worried that it would lunge, flapping, in my direction. I didn't have the sense to think that no matter how splendid, the birds wouldn't last long as faculty emblems if they went around clawing up students.

In my naivety, I didn't appreciate the significance of Brenda's career when I contacted her about my potential thesis. If I had,

I would never have dared. The author of *Poe's Cat* and *The Wing of Night*, deigning to read my stuff?

But she did, and she agreed to be my primary supervisor. She even sympathised with me about the screaming rainbow dinosaurs roaming the grounds.

For three and a half years, Brenda and I met regularly in her vibrant and eclectic office. Our conversations were exhilarating; she was considered, funny and compassionate. When my beloved grandmother died she urged me to take the time I needed, writing that grandmothers are so important and she still dreamed about hers.

I felt the same as Georgia Richter did when first in Brenda's company: 'I moved from undergrad to postgrad, from a girl finding her way to an adult whose opinions were sought and valued.'[1] This graceful, statuesque woman would sit back in her chair, allow a ballet flat to dangle from her foot, and speak to me like a peer. She would read through my drafts, crossing out the overwritten parts, then return them with feedback and questions while I tried to scribble down every word she said.

I loved it, but I struggled with it, too. I was an anxious person, eager to please and not wanting to have my (many) mistakes pointed out to me. So where did I get the gumption to ask, on

1 'Vale Brenda Walker (1957 to 2024)', fremantlepress.com.au/2024/12/13/vale-brenda-walker-1957-to-2024, 13 December 2024.

an early occasion when she drew a sword through one of my fictional darlings, 'Can I keep it for now and see if I can make it work?'

She looked at me, patient, surprised. 'No one's ever asked me that before,' she said.

Of course they hadn't. They shouldn't.

'I promise if you cross it out again, I'll leave it,' I said.

It's a testament to her character that she humoured me. Later, when I reread the material, of course I eliminated the lines Brenda had indicated. She was right. Delia Falconer describes Brenda's own self-editing this way: '[she] was fearless in making swift cuts as she arranged strands of calm unspooling prose.'[2] I was the beneficiary of that talent, and it was finally dawning on me.

Of course, writers should stand by their work and not robotically follow the instructions of an editor, no matter how skilled. But Brenda and I had talked through these issues. I took her treating me as an equal for granted. I was not, and I still am not. But I try. We all try. And now, seventeen years since we first met, as I revise my stories and even when getting down my first drafts, a

---

2 'Remembering Brenda Walker', *The Conversation*, theconversation.com/remembering-brenda-walker-245840, 16 December 2024.

question hovers at my shoulder, as gentle yet powerful as Brenda herself: WWBC, or What Would Brenda Cut? And then I do.

—

Brooke Dunnell is the author of the novels *Last Best Chance* and *The Glass House*, which won the 2021 Fogarty Literary Award.

Tracy Farr – Quietly, fiercely inspirational

I first met Brenda Walker at UWA in 1986, when I returned to study (a mature-age student at twenty-four!) to embark on a BA. Brenda was my first lecturer and tutor in the English Department that year; I feel so lucky to have studied and learned under her throughout the four years of my Arts degree. She was quietly, elegantly, determinedly, fiercely inspirational, motivating me to major in English and to take Women's Studies in 1990 (the first year it was offered at UWA, co-led by Brenda with Delys Bird, if I recall correctly). More than that, though, she inspired me to write.

Our paths didn't cross in person after 1990 (I left Perth the following year, and have lived overseas ever since). She stayed with me, though. One example of this: Brenda is in my diary from July 1990, when she won the Hungerford Prize for *Crush*. I cut out the article and photo – Brenda with Tom Hungerford! – from the *Subiaco Post*, glued it onto the page, marked it and dated it. I've carted that diary from Perth to Vancouver to Aotearoa New Zealand where I now live. I have it on the desk now, beside me as I type.

In 2013 – ever the late starter – my own first novel was published (by Fremantle Press, who had published Brenda's debut). Responding to a ten-questions-type author interview at the time, I wrote, 'The person who inspired me to write was Brenda Walker, who tutored me at university. I first started trying to write the year her first novel, *Crush*, was published (1991). I was equally inspired back then by Elizabeth Jolley, Peter Carey, Helen Garner, Jeanette Winterson, Tim Winton, Beverley Farmer. I wanted to do what they did. I still do.'

As well as driving me to write through her own work, it was through Brenda that I had discovered (or deepened my reading of and love for) so many of the other writers I name-checked then, especially Jolley, Garner and Farmer. My own debt to Brenda is immeasurable.

She will be so very greatly missed, by so many.

T.A.G. Hungerford prize winner Dr Brenda Walker with Tom Hungerford at Fremantle Arts Centre Press.

Sudden inspiration helps make novel a winner

Sudden bursts of inspiration early in the morning and late at night were what helped Brenda Walker write a prize-winning novel.

July 1990
The Subiaco Post

—

Tracy Farr is a writer from Perth, who has lived for nearly thirty years in Aotearoa New Zealand.

Deb Fitzpatrick – Some memories of Brenda Walker

I met Brenda Walker as an undergraduate student at UWA when I was nineteen. She was quietly spoken, wise and kind, and it was through her that I was steered into the fraternity of creative writing in Western Australia.

In 1992, as a third-year student, I took the creative writing unit, English 304, which came with the handmade, spiral-bound resource, *Creative Writing Manual*, a collection of photocopied hand-edited manuscripts, interviews with authors, poets and playwrights, gathered by Brenda and her colleagues Van Ikin and Dennis Haskell. This quickly became my favourite textbook of all my studies, and I still treasure it today. It drew open the curtains on the life of the writer, sharing techniques, struggles and approaches to the craft I could only dream of one day claiming as my own.

That semester I wrote my first – fairly ordinary – short stories. I think I got a B for the unit. I could write, but I couldn't see what I wanted to say. However, I loved the creative pursuit, and I wanted to do better at it.

At the end of the year, Brenda asked me what I was doing the following year. I said I'd been offered entry to honours and was trying to decide on my research topic. 'You know, you can do an honours in creative writing,' she said in her distinctive voice.

That gentle, generous suggestion undoubtedly changed my life.

Thanks to Brenda, I went on to do my honours in creative writing, in which I wrote some slightly better short stories, one of which was published in the literary journal *Imago*. I also wrote a critical essay entitled, 'Images of Perth and Western Australia in Robert Drewe's *The Bodysurfers* and Brenda Walker's *Crush*'. Brenda's writing had a massive effect on my own:

In *Crush*, we are privy to Beaufort Street, Limbo's nightclub, L'Alba Café, Hyde Park – real places which provide for plausible and interesting settings in fiction. Without writers like Walker […] I would not have felt confident in setting stories in Perth …

After some years working and travelling, I returned to my beloved UWA English Department where Brenda, Van and Dennis still were, like family, and I undertook my masters in creative writing. In 2010 my first novel was published, and 2025 will mark the publication of my tenth novel. I have many people to thank for my career, but Brenda began the thought of it.

My heartfelt condolences to her family on the loss of this beautiful woman.

—

Deb Fitzpatrick is an award-winning writer of fiction and creative non-fiction for readers of all ages.

Amy Fleet – Her room, for us, a sturdy boat

I couldn't believe my fortune when the university offered up a creative writing course. Brenda Walker was going to be my tutor. We gathered outside her room in the hallway and her door was open. We filed in and she stood to the left, looking like a graceful, long-necked subject of a painting. She was a published author by then and I was again in disbelief that I was under her tutelage, feeling very young and unsophisticated. She looked at us with kind brown eyes and over the weeks, I found myself watching for her shockingly beautiful smile to appear when someone read out something amusing. Her voice was smooth and the words she spoke, so light and soft yet to the point. She was powerful in a gentle way. I'd never met a woman like that. I had spent my undergraduate years being a bit of a clown and Brenda managed to treat me seriously enough that I began to see past my own facade. It was a huge turning point. I felt clumsy and invisible growing up, writing to make people laugh at me, but suddenly I was in the company of someone who had self-respect and enormous creative drive.

One day, I'd like to be a writer, I had thought. Brenda showed me that the time was not one day, but now. I stepped into my shoes the day she put her head to the side and said, 'You know your style reminds me of someone I've been reading lately. Have you read her work?' I hadn't, but I rode my bike home through Kings Park, elated that she had mentioned I have a writing style! I was off to find all the books I could read. Brenda Walker taught me to listen to others in my tute group with excited objectivity. I couldn't wait for her weekly class. I had become a better searcher, listener and moved past the self-consciousness one can face when sharing writing with a group. Brenda created a working space where we could feel like we were enough. Her room was a birthing suite for our raw ideas. She had an eye for beauty. I could tell by the way her books were on the shelves … the posy of flowers, the appreciation for visual calm. She invited the sunlight to touch her desk. I was at first a brassy, messy, loud girl, regarded by her, a goddess, who found words potent and precious: who despite my youth and tardiness, reminded me that I also contained potency and ability. Her grace has come with me thirty years on. I see her eyes holding my shy face up in the light of that morning room, gently saying it's not just ok, but it is essential to step into your own credibility as a woman who writes.

—

Amy Fleet, double English major at UWA 1989–1993, has been an English teacher, writer and tram conductor in Victoria.

Alan Fyfe – Deuteronomy 2:27

I will write the truth here, without adding or subtracting anything – excepting any subtractions that make what I write into a better story. 'Always know more than you put on the page'[1] is something I heard in Brenda Walker's class. It may not be her original phrase, but that was the first place I heard someone articulate this immutable foundation of good narrative. Think of *Tristram Shandy*, where the joke is that trying to convey every detail of the truth will smother the very possibility of a story. It's funny, and the gag works because 'always know more than you put on the page' is right and true.

Maybe that rings like a cliché but Brenda was never a clichéd thinker. It takes a kind of guru to understand exactly what cliché is and what is truism, and Brenda was a kind of guru. She was entirely right because this autobiographical note, as much as I am the author, is about what is happening in your imagination. Of course, Brenda put it better than I can. On *The Decameron*, she notes '*This book is a reminder that the storyteller doesn't have a monopoly on the exercise of the imagination; it's based on the understanding that the reader is a storyteller-in-waiting*'.[2]

---

1 All quotes from Brenda Walker are from conversations, or from her memoir, *Reading by Moonlight: How books saved a life* (Penguin, 2010), which she was writing then redrafting when I studied with her.

2 Brenda Walker, *Reading by Moonlight*, p. 191.

And here's me with my *avant* demeanour like a fifty-two-year-old teenager – and there's Brenda at the distance of almost twenty years past the day we met we met, and her whole life lived and gone.

And there you are, out past the barrier of the page, the storyteller-in-waiting. Waiting patiently (or not so patiently) through this preamble to bring Brenda and my interactions to life in your mind, to fill gaps and colour in the blanks and grow a world around variances of twenty-six letter symbols that mean nothing but what we invest in them.

Yet I exist too, not just by an act of what Barthes called '*filiation*', where readers reflexively connect writers to their work, but a real human tapping at the keys of a laptop one unseasonably cool morning in Bayswater, on a December in 2024. This can never only be you in the privacy of silent reading – it is a social act between you and another real human being, with each of us contributing our imaginative part like separate voices in a harmony.

This real human being, with his own pains and preferences, with his own willingness to share and his own vault of secrets you'll never know, is thinking about Brenda. He is incredibly sad at her loss and will always be sad at it. He is incredibly happy that he got to meet her and learn from her. He is incredibly grateful that she changed everything for him.

~

The first thing I'll leave out are the people and circumstances that stopped me going to university in my twenties. You'll find me at the local sandstone in my early thirties, doing very well as a student after a shaky start in first semester where I started, then dropped out of, a communications degree – permanently casting aside the illusion that this education binge was ever about a proper job, and wilfully making myself unemployable with a double major in literature and philosophy. I've come to university to become the writer that I've wanted to be since I was thirteen: a maker of stories and poems.

Meanwhile, as I'm averaging over 90 in Cultural Studies, the rest of my life is falling apart. My finances, my marriage, my family, and all my sureties will go under for this single-minded goal. I see it as survival – it feels as though I need to complete this degree or give up on life. The people closest to me try to understand but I can never explain it to their satisfaction. That's the first hard truth about how to be an artist, you must be a little bit selfish. Not a monster, it can be done without becoming a monster, and Brenda is proof of that, but your ego and ambition should run towards the prize and not be turned aside.

Which is another thing I hear from Brenda. I go to a John Kinsella lecture and, among the complex geometry of the way John delivers his communications, a little cynicism slips out: 'Let's face it, who gets published depends on who goes to which dinner parties with whom.' And I believe this, because I'm already seeing it happen around me – big chances going to people doing nothing to earn them. The world is like this, and I've never actually been to a dinner party.

I repeat John's assertion later in Brenda's tutorial, but I can't quite square it up with our mutual admiration for Kim Scott's *Benang: From the Heart* because I've discovered this novel written by someone from the state where I was born and raised that feels, to me, like true genius – the kind of writing that is undeniable no matter what secret handshakes passed between attendees at bourgeois dinner parties.

Brenda doesn't disagree with John, but she adds that she doesn't think it is a universal. She believes that 'Surely there are some artists, like Kim Scott, who turn neither left nor right.' These words are a memorable counterpoint and are, again, true; words John left off the page during his lecture that round out a whole truth about being an artist. You can network, sure, or you can be in the right place at the right time, you can be the right kind of photogenic or speak in the tones of the right socio-economic grouping.

But you can also do the work. You can work diligently and obsessively until what you do becomes undeniable. The truth needn't always be the worst case. Around the truth's hard-cut edges there can be a gem-like gleam of inspiration too. Brenda knows this: as with any great storyteller, she knows what to include and what to leave out. It's one of several times she tells me the story of what I can be.

~

To be transparent, me discovering Kim Scott isn't exactly the way it happens. Rather, I'm introduced to Kim Scott in the first of Brenda's units I enrol for – Australian literature. *Benang: From the Heart* is one of many formative texts put in front of me under Brenda Walker's curation. There, and across other units she established, I read *The Corrections*, *Giovanni's Room*, and *Hiam*. I have Charmain Clift, PiO, Dorothy Hewett, and Miranda July as set texts. I learn the bizarre story Haruki Murakami tells about suddenly deciding to be a novelist while watching a baseball game (which I doubt) and read Jonathan Franzen arguing that the social novel is a dead form (which I also doubt).[3]

In her honours level novel writing unit, I critique the painfully long first sentence of *Atonement*, already having made it a rule (gleaned from a writing a little journalism) that first sentences

---

3 Murakami became one of my favourite novelists, but I have always been highly dubious that such a complex and involved writer of fiction just spontaneously started writing novels with no previous ambition, practice, or planning (as he claims in his introduction to *Wind Pinball: Two novels*). This story sounds suspiciously like the kind of whimsical magic realism he writes and is typical of the impulse most good storytellers have, to make everything into a cool story. Feel free to love storytellers, but never fully trust us. Franzen is also a writer I enjoy, but the tired hipster points he makes about the social novel being dead (killed by TV apparently, which sounds a bit like old-man Adorno and his aversion to jazz) in his 1996 essay, 'Perchance to Dream', can be destroyed by the usual Socratic method of finding any good modern social novel – of which there are quite a few. Still, Franzen's weird assumption highlights a problem with literary studies which is, no matter the student, it's impossible to read everything. Every new book we encounter contains the delicious possibility that it might destroy our preconceptions.

shouldn't be over twenty-three words long. Brenda likes Ian McEwan in a way that I never will, but she nods approvingly as I talk about great first sentences nonetheless, because I have picked up a writing technique and I am applying it.

In that first unit on Australian literature, though, Brenda is not my tutor. She is a distant figure at the other end of the lecture hall where I regularly sit near the back and learn how experts explaining their thoughts on books can be the most entertaining thing in the world.

She lectures as a storyteller, building arcs of history, ideas, and images into her analysis. Thoroughly modern in the days when several professors haven't figured out their way past overhead projectors, Brenda intersperses her PowerPoint slides with photographs and graphic material, understanding the intricacies of the visual in combination with the written word. She has a stillness, yet her voice has something related to performance poetry in it. Creative writers know, after all, that words carry more than information to the hearer, they are also vehicles for emotion. Humour is never her main tool, but she is always ready for humour and waiting to catch it in the net of her oration if the opportunity comes around.

At the end of the unit, Brenda calls me into her office to pick up my final essay. I haven't yet met this impressive lecturer in person, and I immediately assume I'm in trouble. I don't have much experience of going into offices when the reason isn't that I'm in trouble. I wrote on Nicholas Jose's *The Red Thread*, approaching the idea that there was a Daoist philosophy stamped on the text.[4] The idea is my own and there has been nothing in the unit readings to suggest that line of research. I think I must have finally overstepped the bounds and done something too silly to be within the field of study I'm pursuing.

I'm not in trouble. Brenda gives back the 5,000 or so printed words standing up and holding the stack of paper in two hands – a gesture which is the opposite of casual. She leans down to make eye contact (she is taller than me) and says 'Well, you've topped the class for marks. Your tutor and I read your essay with such pleasure. This isn't the work of the student, this is like the work of a colleague, and a *really* good one.' In the next moment she's leading me through the halls, printing a photocopy for herself and calling through a doorway at another staff member, 'What prizes can we enter this for?'

She asks me a lot of questions about my philosophy studies, which I can barely remember. She tells me I have talent, which I appreciate. She enjoins me to keep going, so I do.

4 *The Red Thread* is a novel that is intimately connected to a Chinese classic, *Six Records of a Floating Life* by Shen Fu – and if you're going to read one, I strongly suggest you allow yourself the pleasure of reading the other, which I did immediately after closing *The Red Thread*. Another way of understanding the vast world behind the tiny signposts that can be included in good narrative is to know that every book leads to other books, and those into other books still, and so on into near infinity.

~

I take every creative writing unit I can under the impressive cohort of authors who teach at the University of Western Australia in the early 2000s – Dennis Haskell, John Kinsella, Van Ikin, and Brenda herself. There are many creative writing units, and I don't understand what a privileged time and place I've landed in to learn the craft.

Neither do I understand fully that creative writing at UWA is very much a house that Brenda built. Her importance there, and worldwide, as a pioneer of creative writing as an academic field doesn't click until I'm talking to a German exchange student one day, who asks if Brenda Walker still works there.

I tell him that her office is only a couple of hundred meters from where we are standing smoking cigarettes by the bay. I figure he must be a fan of her novels and ask him if that's the case, but it's her reputation as a creative writing teacher that he knows and that awes him. He explains that nothing like the courses I take are available in the universities he has access to back in Germany, and that many people craving to learn writing in other countries know the reputation of Brenda Walker.

Not that her reputation matters to me, I have already decided to follow her teaching as closely as possible. By the time I get to do her honours unit, I have my own reputation as a student writer of promise and my life has further disintegrated. My wife and

I have separated, and I don't have a stable place to live. I have already become irresponsible with drug use.

But I maintain. I turn up sober and keen at every class and I do my study diligently no matter where I find myself for the night. This is what I came for – the higher secrets of the artform, which Brenda delivers with abundance. Every seminar is filled with terminology and techniques. This is the advanced toolbox of writing, and I am soaking it all in, adopting every maxim and theory into my private self. There, I encounter Martha Nussbaum's elegant thinking for the first time, and Brenda explains how she uses it. I am able to give names to dozens of the things I already do in my writing and harness them into intentionality. I learn dozens more techniques I would have never guessed at too.

My first presentation in class comes and I have arrogantly picked a very strange way of writing a story, trying to fuse poetry into the narrative with even paragraphs like formal stanzas. Some of the other students are confused by the structure, and Brenda isn't sure it's a working proposition either. But she narrows her eyes, holding the paper up in front of her and says, 'The prose is incredibly strong though.'

For my next presentation, I've worked out a better story, which will be my final assignment for the unit. The other students respond well this time, smiling and generous with their feedback, exactly in the way of literature diehards who've encountered a piece of writing that gives them pleasure to read. Brenda has the paper laid on the table in front of her this time, her gestures are more open and relaxed than at the last presentation, and she says with conviction, 'Everyone's talking about Craig Silvey's prose at the moment. This, to me, is far better.'[5]

My life outside of study is in near-catastrophic overload by the end of the unit. I hand in my story late and at twice the word limit. I discuss with Brenda that it is going over the limit and she tells me some things just have to be seen through to the end. I pick up my final assignment in the usual way, from a drop box with no call to the office. It has two sentences of feedback, which are entirely complimentary, and a mark of 90, which I see Brenda has marked down from 93 – I had to be penalised some way, I suppose. Not that it feels like a penalty. Enough has been said.

After three years, I find a place to rent long-term by the river in Pinjarra. It's not a pleasant place. Holes are punched in the asbestos walls and there is Satanic graffiti from a previous tenant left in one of the rooms – the house has no cooking equipment installed either. It's a private arrangement with a kind of slum lord, someone quite famous who would sue me if I dropped his name. I ask for nothing, he doesn't charge me much and doesn't move me on, that's the deal. I clean myself up because I must – I now have majority care of my son.

5 Apologies to Craig Silvey: this was Brenda's claim, not mine.

I try to fit as much work in as I can between looking after my boy. I have no TV connected and I don't care to watch it anyway. All my spare time is spent on writing, reading and learning. Apart from a great friendship with an American poetry editor called Michelle Greenblatt, carried out online and over the phone, nothing much moves with my writing career. I diligently submit to Australian journals, and no one pays attention. I keep working at it anyway. Trying to improve, trying to become undeniable.

Those seasons feel very desperate, and I get into a lot of despair over a near publishing standstill that lasts eight years. In the middle of it, I don't know what to do other than reach out to Brenda, wondering if she even remembers me.

She does remember me very clearly and we exchange a few emails. She asks what I'm reading. I talk about how I have gotten deeply into John Shaw Neilson and about the connection between his poem 'The Orange Tree' and the pictorial symbol of the Scottish Presbyterian Church he was a member of – the burning bush with the Latin motto *nec tamen consumebatur*. Brenda says she knows the symbol well, having grown up around 'that stern faith', and that she loves the message of resilience it entails.[6]

---

6 The English translation of *nec tamen consumebatur* is 'it is not consumed'. I didn't realise how many times my conversations with Brenda referenced Moses until I wrote this essay. She was well across Biblical literature, another excellent foundation for a creative writer, regardless of belief.

It's a small thing, just someone who knows about reading and writing to talk to. She is head of English now and entirely busy due to the beginning of the deep staff and funding cuts that will eventually gut the arts at UWA and other Australian universities. Her illnesses have caught up with her again too. She apologises for not being able to offer more of her time, but it feels like a lot to me; and it's more discussion of writing than I've had in years.

I get back to work. If no one is going to listen, I will write volumes anyway. I turn neither left nor right. I burn yet I am not consumed.

❧

Slowly, people do start to listen though. Journals start to show interest in my stories and poems. New mentors come into my life, foremost among them Lucy Dougan, who shows the first flourish of convinced praise from an editor at a major Australian journal. New friends in writing bring back that special glow to the craft that Brenda had imbued it with. I find the love of my life and move in with her to a rental bungalow Maylands where we fuse families. I have a good place to live (with installed cooking equipment).

The best thing that ever happens to me comes next – the bottom falls out of the industry I'm working in, and I lose my job. Without hesitation, I sit down to write a novel. I use all of Brenda's methods – chapter plan, timeline, draft and distance and redraft. 'I never feel safe until I'm nine thousand words in', she said. I set nine thousand words as a goal and, once I'm past that hump, keep working. I use characters and narratives from two short stories drafted in Brenda's creative writing units to build the world of the novel.

I redraft four times; Brenda said it wouldn't be easy to arrive at the final work, so I feel like I expected this. I get the interest, then lose the interest, of several publishers. One publisher loses funding when they're just about to publish the book. I turn neither left nor right and redraft three more times. The novel is published, listed for several awards, and receives acclaim in every review.

I return to UWA to undertake a PhD. Brenda has retired by now, but I find others with helping hands and wisdom of their own. I learn about funding opportunities and set out to become a full-time writer, and it happens. I get everything I wanted.

As I publish more and, in the style of being a working writer in the 2020s, announce each little success on social media, Brenda follows me, keeping up with everything I do and dropping a demure *like* reaction on every step forward. I get the chance to tell her what her teaching meant to me, and I hope she feels a little pride in it. Though I am very far from the only source of pride she has in that department. Our national literature, and all its plaudits, is woven through with the names of Brenda Walker's former students.

Sometimes, out of nostalgia for my busking days, I post a video of myself online playing an instrument and singing. I do Dylan's

'Boots of Spanish Leather' for a new year message and Brenda comments 'beautiful'. In my mind, I go back to my undergrad days getting a high distinction from Professor Walker. Another little thing, perhaps, but enough little things piled together can stand very high.

~

I do some sessional teaching now. When I say I have everything I wanted ... well, you can always want a bit more – I'm not wealthy, or even middle-class comfortable, not yet. I'm getting by on funding, and some teaching back at the Sandstone helps pay the power bills.

I think of Brenda when I'm teaching even more than when I wrote my first book. Every time I take students through terminology for a technique and its meaning, some of her voice is with me. She didn't teach everything I know now, but she did give me keys to learn a great deal of it. When I talk about free indirect speech, or the pathetic fallacy, or take students through the complex process of building voice in prose fiction, I'm back in that room on the first floor of the Arts Building for Brenda's evening classes. That foundation, plus 'yesterday's seven-thousand years',[7] and I'm not too bad a teacher.

---

7 Paraphrased from stanza XX of Edward FitzGerald's translation of Omar Khayyam.

The classes are bigger, the cohort of writing teachers is smaller, the pay is near criminal and, in a recent legal ruling, was genuinely found to be criminal in several cases. But the students still respond to assured and exact knowledge often enough, and they respond to genuine enthusiasm for the craft too.

I tell them about the difficulties of publishing anything in the world as it is now, about my story and how none of it is easy. I tell them that sometimes they'll see the inherent corruption of people being rewarded fabulously for doing almost no work. That publishing, like the rest of the world, is a field that can be classist, racist, sexist, backwards thinking, limited, and eminently wrong about everything concerning art. I tell them that the work means something though. I'm a writer and I can put things into different words, but I'm saying to them that if you still want it after all those obstacles are taken into consideration, you must take the path and turn neither left nor right.

Most importantly, if I find students who are very good at writing, or who becomes good under my tutelage, I tell them. I find a quiet moment and a space where they can take it in, and I tell them that they are good and that they can have a life of art if they want it. I know what that telling can mean in the hardest times.

~

Lucy calls me two months after the end of another semester of teaching and she tells me about Brenda's accident the day before, the day of Emily Dickinson's birthday and my own, and that my teacher is no longer with us. I'm standing outside, by my front door, and I sink down to a little stool that supports my sore, middle-aged body folding into a crouch. I smoke and cry a while. The world takes on a low, sick hum.

❧

Maybe you are trained in literature too, and you can pick out some of the intentions and techniques that hold this piece of writing together. You might have seen the conventions of bildungsroman, or you may wonder what feeling I'm trying to manipulate you into with present-tense phrasing. I have written longer than I had intended. It is late afternoon, and the first draft (which you will never read in the original – who would dishonour this memory with a first draft?) has taken one full workday. It came out easily because there are many things I want to say about Brenda.

There is a lot I have left out about her. I have centred on her teaching and academic life, but her writing was an integral part of who she was too. Many discussions have been had about that writing, and many more will be had in times to come. Aviva Tuffield, writing for *Australian Book Review*, reveals how Brenda's maxim of conveying a larger world by knowing all there was to know about it, but telling only a little, was executed on the pages of *The Wing of Night:*

> *This historical novel has clearly emerged from extensive research, yet it does not try to parade its knowledge or to bombard the reader with military details. It is*

not concerned with painting the big picture of the war but of sketching the specific experiences of a handful of characters. Walker signals her intentions early with her epigram from a story by Henry James: 'My own taste has always been for unwritten history and my present business is with the reverse of the picture.' And so, although there are interludes on the battlefield, Walker's emphasis is on the lesser-known tales of Australian rural life during wartime, and on the travails of the damaged soldiers on their return. The focus is always close-up on the lives, thoughts, emotions, and voices of a few individuals, creating a sense, in true Jamesian fashion, of 'felt life'.[8]

Tuffield's review demonstrates, also, how closely Brenda's teaching and creative life were enmeshed. She could practise everything she preached and use every technique she explained. I can't add much to the critics who have extensively praised her writing. What I can offer is a story about Brenda's extraordinary humanity and warmth, and how effective that approach was in teaching and in lifting fellow artists.

I nod with recognition when Georgia Richter writes of beginning her masters degree under Brenda's supervision: *'As we talked, it began to dawn on me with a slow kind of wonder that Brenda*

---

8 Aviva Tuffield, 'The Reverse of the Picture', *Australian Book Review*, No. 277, December 2005, australianbookreview.com.au/abr-online/archive/2005/258-december-2005-january-2006/12407-aviva-tuffield-reviews-the-wing-of-night-by-brenda-walker.

was speaking to me as if I was already a colleague of hers' and that '*Brenda did not ask for vulnerability without giving it in return*.'[9] There are many great writers in the world, not all of them can mould other artists so successfully, fewer still can do so with such kindness.

There is more I have left out about myself – about addiction, about mental health, about ideation, and about the histories and causes for these things. But that is apt. We end by circling back to the beginning of the work (as all stories should), and we remember that the art of narrative is equally divided between what is included and what is unsaid.

You might find some of what I left out of this piece if you read my other works, either frankly admitted in confessional poetry or as experience filtered through prose fiction. If you do so, it is due to the immense privilege I have of publishing my chosen artform for the public and seeing it placed in bookstores and libraries. This privilege is because of my training under fine teachers as much as it is to do with any qualities that are native to myself.

If you have never met me in person, I exist only in this arrangement of twenty-six meaningless letter symbols, which you have made meanings from. You have engaged in that process Brenda was explaining when she wrote about finding the right books to save yourself from the abyss:

---

9 'Vale Brenda Walker (1957 to 2024)', fremantlepress.com.au/2024/12/13/vale-brenda-walker-1957-to-2024, 13 December 2024.

> *We each have one life, one share of action and vision and money: a single life for all our speech and thought, our decent gestures and the decisions that might undo us, our welcome or unwanted love, our parties that may or may not come off. One life to satisfy our vast and human sense of voyaging. With the right books we find out what imaginary strangers have done with their share of this amazing thing, life.*[10]

Writing this, I become that imaginary stranger to you.

Still, if you attend closely to all the things that are left out, if you lean in to make eye contact (I am only the height of a page to you, so you must be taller), you might see the furious activity that happens in the white spaces between the rows of letter symbols. Look very closely and you may glimpse the slight and opaque outlines of a life being saved.

—

Alan Fyfe is a writer of stories and poems from WA. He is the author of a novel, *T* (Transit Lounge, 2022), and a book of poetry, *G-d, Sleep, and Chaos* (Gazebo, 2024).

10 Brenda Walker, *Reading by Moonlight*, p. 4.

Brenda Glover – Brenda Walker

I became acquainted with Brenda Walker in 2003 when she was an examiner for my PhD thesis in English Literature and Creative Writing. Her report was generous and constructive, much appreciated. We stayed in touch and I subsequently met with her at book launches and award functions.

I remember Brenda for her elegance, eloquence, kindness and generosity to all she associated with. She gave freely of her time to other writers. Her own writing resonated with her readers.

Brenda was a wonderful woman and she will be sorely missed. My deepest sympathy goes to her family, friends and colleagues.

—

Brenda Glover is a literary/writing academic, a cultural theorist whose PhD thesis was examined by Brenda Walker.

Dennis Haskell – The sirens

i.m. Brenda Walker

I go out early
and the streets hold
only a scatter of joggers,
owners walked by their dogs,
the hazily sleepless, and urging hands
queued at café coffee counters.

By mid-morning, 37 degrees
and rising, heat has captured
those same streets, but people
skitter between cars, the cafés
are thriving, and shoppers
starting to get Christmas-desperate
head to air-conditioned malls.
In the near distance, sirens
like the wailing of wounded animals
have little to do with us;

but, eating a late lunch,
I get the call: a friend,
a breast cancer survivor
and so careful of her health,
was out for her morning walk

when a breakneck hack of a driver
hit her, crossing the road
near the park she loved so well.
Her parents lived into their 90s
and I used to joke with her
how her genes promised a long life;
now one reckless idiot
has stolen all those years.

Life keeps up its unpredictable
appointments with the sudden dark
and you must, must ask not
for whom the sirens wail.

—

Dennis Haskell taught with Brenda at UWA and she made sure he was in the audience for her first conference paper.

Yasmin Haskell – Guest room

in memory of Brenda Walker

'Hygge', you wrote, 'the mind can travel',
From Oslo, I think, you sent the scream socks.
I'd wear them to meetings, we joked.

And I played arabesques at your flat, with
Anton cavorting and Sophie souffléed –
Such pretending to write, such cloud of cat!

But now I must hasten to *you* along
That sad avenue of soaring gums,
And float above the shrine and peer

Down on the wide smile of the Swan.
'You can see my path from here', we joked,
'I can wave at you, from South Perth!'

Your bed is made up.
The birds are lifting from the river.
Meet you under the dragon's blood tree.

—

Yasmin Haskell was Brenda's close friend and former colleague. She was excited about Brenda visiting her in Melbourne in the new year.

Sarah Hay – A conversation, postponed

In the week before Brenda died, we'd planned to catch up, have coffee. Like we'd done so many times before. It would be another small moment, insignificant at the time, that would form part of our larger story. In the early years of our friendship, some thirty years ago, we recounted the intimacies of our daily lives almost as they occurred. These moments buoyed us, kept us afloat in the wash of life's challenges and disappointments. We gave each other advice, saved snippets to discuss, news of the mundane to world events; from the absurd to the practical. Most of all, we laughed. We read each other's writing; celebrated each other's wins. In the last decade or so, life events affected the flow of our narrative. A marriage, and in my case, a change in career. We no longer lived streets away. The flow was episodic, and it relied on a greater commitment. Days before Brenda's death, I was driving to my home on the south coast. Our coffee date had slipped away unnoticed. As I drove, I thought of phoning. Talking as the words ate up the kilometres. But I'd just entered a black spot. No matter, I thought, I'll call her when I get home. I'll find a time when the sun is warm, settle into my favourite chair, the birds will be out, Brenda will comment on their singing, and we'll talk about our writing; the progress we were making. We'd make plans for another time; another adventure; another moment. There was so much to talk about.

—

Sarah Hay is a lawyer and award-winning author of *Skins* (Allen & Unwin, 2002) and *Texas: An Australian Love Story* (Allen & Unwin, 2008).

Paul Hetherington – Opening out: in memory of Brenda Walker

There are many ways to talk of friendship – the boon of knowing another in surprising ways; the residual force of occasional connections that resonate though a life, although lightly made and held. Such matters are often explored in poetry, and they are especially part of the province of poetry made in worlds where human connections are easily disrupted by distance or changing circumstance. Usually such poetry is lyrical, finding in language's beguiling rhythms the ineffable appeal of meeting and understanding another person.

These issues are in the inimitable poetry of Sappho, for example, and much of the poetry of China's golden age, the T'ang Dynasty. They are also in a good deal of the lyric poetry of the English Renaissance. A characteristic scenario is that two people come together to share a rite of passage or social activity. There is a reciprocity between them; a familiarity. They part. There may be no definite prospect of spending time together again.

The connection may be light, but these people have been moved – embraced, as it were, by the idea of another. They may take on part of the spirit of the other, often without much thought. This may occur in much the same way as an encounter with an enticing breeze that, afterwards, the body never forgets.

They may correspond. One person may feel enmeshed and the other walk away from that small sphere of influence only faintly touched by it. Perhaps what most matters about such occasions is the opportunity for genuinely productive, even creative human connection; and the hope it provides that the better parts of the human condition will not wither in the face of cynicism, grandstanding, and so much else that human beings continually do.

And such encounters may largely be composed of small gestures and fleeting impressions. For instance, it is 1984 and an elegant, self-possessed woman is in the corridor of the English Department at the University of Western Australia. She introduces herself as Brenda Walker and it is as if, almost whimsically, she opens a sense of brightness.

Soon we are part of occasional meetings where contract and sessional lecturers and tutors, PhD candidates and honours students chat about their research and teaching, or simply take brief refuge together from the demands of work. Sometimes we discuss our creative writing. We are all teachers or students of what is now called literary studies but was then referred to as English literature and, in the more informal of these meetings, literature encounters the quotidian and the contemporary – including ideas of feminism, gender and what Kimberlé Crenshaw subsequently called intersectionalism – and in these contexts, books come alive, awakening into conversation.

We are aware that there are many academics employed in the English literature discipline, so prospects for further work look reasonably good.

Brenda and I continue to chat. She is not so much shy as occasionally diffident – or so it seems – and, also, from time to time refreshingly assertive. She loves Samuel Beckett's writing, including its directness and capacity to deal with deep existential issues with a dark humorousness. More generally, she enjoys framing her thinking in terms of her reading. She is highly accomplished intellectually, observant, frequently amusing, sometimes wry, and skilled at negotiating with the male academics and their egos.

I suspect she has creative ambitions, too, in a way she does not fully disclose. Her prose style is remarkably fine – suggestive, spare, evocative, telling. I complete my honours year and enrol in a masters degree, which soon becomes a PhD and I teach on a sessional basis. From time to time, Brenda and I cross paths in the English Department and occasionally reflect together, rather mordantly, on the strangeness of academic life.

She and I don't often meet after I leave Perth in 1990. However, I sometimes drop in to see her in her UWA office when I return to the city, and she is always warm, inviting and thoughtful. When she chooses to be, she is scintillating. Her creative writing flourishes, she publishes a series of highly impressive and superbly poised novels, one of which is shortlisted for the

Miles Franklin Literary Award, and a beautiful memoir in which reading is central. She is eventually appointed to a professorship.

Not so many years ago she visited me in the ACT. I left my campus at the University of Canberra, and we met and drank at the Australian National University Bar. We discussed writing and reading, politics, the world economy and a great deal else. Once again, it was there, as in the tutorial rooms so many decades previously – a sense of connection; the possibility that ideas have wide implications and might be remembered in the body; and a concomitant opening out of generosity.

—

Paul Hetherington is Emeritus Professor of Writing at the University of Canberra and has published eighteen full-length poetry collections.

Gail Jones – Brenda Walker

In Brenda's meditation on illness and books, *Reading By Moonlight*, she mentions an art installation. Ken Unsworth's *In the Shadow of Stars* is a work of mourning, constructed in tribute to the artist's wife. It features a hospital bed in a darkened room and a collection of pale moving lights, a kind of inkling of stars. 'It wasn't a sombre place,' writes Brenda, 'it was loving.'

This is perhaps the spirit in which, borrowing her spirit and her wisdom, we might think about Brenda's passing. She leaves behind pale, moving lights against the darkness. Her words and quality of self remain in those who knew her, or lived with her, or read her words, and this trace serves us all as a persistent and loving gift.

—

Gail Jones is a former colleague of Brenda's from the University of Western Australia and a fiction writer, now based in Sydney.

John Kinsella – Elegy for Brenda Walker (1957–2024)

Memoir

in memory of Brenda Walker

(i)

Out walking
the relative cool

of the morning
and discussing

day's unfolding
with the magpie tiding,

the loss of a friend
emanates

from the bush
of Kaarta Koomba

and follows the river
up over The Scarp,

traces river, brook,
and dry 'winter creek'

to inflect so many
conversations

on writing, on how
to make a way

through memoir
and remember

all we have passed,
all we will sense.

(ii)

In discussing
the possibilities

of fiction
when *Crush*

appeared
in a city

retuning
or resetting

under Moreton Bay
figs in Hyde Park,

we extended
the conversation

across immediate
years

to the poetics
of death

and how much
we were both

going to make life
work the best

way possible,
whatever

the circumstances,
the conditions.

(iii)

This agreement
we had

about one day
meeting

on a street
in New York,

just to pass
and say 'hi'

and keep
on going

towards
the lives

we were writing
into other

versions
of a story.

Or the agreement
not to say

anything after
you had a word

with authorities
to free me

from the lock-up
after my protest

to release
incarcerated animals

from their pain.
You merged

in and out of the shadows,
but always there

if called upon.
Not often, sometimes.

(iv)

So generous
when Tracy and I

married, to offer
a plate whose design

was a mandala,
an exposition

to the building
of a friendship

that could follow
the shifts

and resolve
however long

between messages,
catching up

even briefly.
We so delighted

in your next life, your
deep bonds.

(v)

Out walking
the relative cool

of the morning
and discussing

day's unfolding
with the magpie tiding,

your wry, friendly
glance of knowing

replaces
a harsh sun

with a warmth
of insight

to what's not working
and how it might

be made whole.
An impossible day.

Remember Iggy and the Stooges
playing riparian static?

Not your music,
but you listened anyway.

Remember Cambridge,
the river that could be drained.

Then later. Much later.
Peppermint tea. Another

river pushing
down to the sea,

but also looking back
over its shoulder.

Then different oceans
away from your

recovery, though
reconnecting,

through memoir
which was your course

I shared. Different
and the same. How

we make stories.
And where. And when.

—

John Kinsella is a poet, critic, fiction writer and environmental activist.

Jeri Kroll – Common bonds

When I first met Brenda decades ago, we realised that we had both written doctorates on Samuel Beckett. That intellectual bond became a personal one in 2011. I had read her wonderful memoir *Reading by Moonlight* and when I too was diagnosed with cancer I contacted her. She responded with a kindness I will never forget, not only answering all my questions but calling me weekly as I negotiated surgery and treatment. She was a compassionate human being as well as a superb writer.

—

Jeri Kroll is Emeritus Professor of English and Creative Writing at Flinders University.

Julia Lawrinson – Kindness

I was always aware of Brenda Walker and her presence from when I entered the writing community in the early 90s. I admit to being slightly intimidated by her at first, by her poise and eloquence and model-esque presence as much as by her beautiful prose, but this intimidation did not survive once I was introduced to her. I was never Brenda's student, but she was nevertheless always hugely generous to me, asking what I was working on and genuinely interested in my career trajectory.

More recently, she was warmly receptive to my entry into the (sometimes terrifying) world of memoir-writing, and she was an early subscriber to my Substack. She sent me a note in January telling me how much she was enjoying my posts, and praising the 'clean clear writing' and 'adroit management of disclosure'; later, just as I was having a nervous breakdown about that same disclosure, she sent me a lovely message about 'your entirely engrossing memoir'. To have someone of Brenda's writing status say such things was such a huge honour, and so affirming. She has given me a model of how to be as a writer, always building community, and I hope to always be as encouraging to others as she was. Kindness begets kindness.

—

Julia Lawrinson is a writer of books for young people, and a memoirist.

Brigid Lowry – Farewell

The campus. The peacocks. The trees. You in your office, my masters' supervisor. Elegant, smart, funny. We talked more about hats, marriages, books and food than my thesis, as I recall, but I got the degree. I went to dinner at your house where I met your son, and was very impressed by the meal, which involved roasted fennel. Later I was delighted to see the lovely photos of your second wedding.

Brenda, your work was beautifully woven, full of truth, authenticity and intelligence. You encouraged so many of us on our inky journeys.

You and I often ran into each other locally, and had little interchanges on the run, about our work, our sons, and which prawns to buy for Christmas. You were a true original. Now you are gone, and I send every blessing to your family at this truly sad time.

—

Brigid Lowry is an author of YA fiction, essay collections and poetry.

Carol Major – Brenda Walker

Brenda was my teacher at University of Technology Sydney some years ago. She was everything that was gracious and learned and gentle with writers' fragile hearts. She held mine and that hand will always be there.

—

Carol Major is a writer and a writing mentor at Varuna, The National Writers' House.

Linda Martin – Brenda Walker

Brenda was a beautiful and passionate writer who made an enormous impact on the WA literary community – not only through her literary works and teachings, but also through her support of and belief in people. I remain grateful to her for giving me the opportunity to tutor for the UWA English Department, and for the many wonderful conversations and laughs we shared in her office. My deepest sympathy to her family.

—

Linda Martin is co-publisher at Night Parrot Press.

Alistair McCartney – Dear Brenda: fragment

Dear Brenda, how to say what you meant to me, and how, like everyone, I was so shocked and saddened to hear of your untimely passing? All I can offer are some fragments, which is how I comprehend the world; I think you would understand.

I remember you lecturing at UWA, teaching me Barthes, *Mythologies*, the difference between the signifier and the signified. Duras too, *The Lover*. You were so cool, so elegant, precise, austere, in your lecturing style and your prose. I heard you read from *Crush*, your first novel, mythologising Northbridge and Mount Lawley and Hyde Park so beautifully, that lost bohemia of the 1980s and 1990s. I have a copy of that in my home in Los Angeles. You were my first creative writing professor and, for someone filled with doubt and uncertainty about their abilities, you gave me so much encouragement in our tutorials in the Arts Building, teaching me to not care if I didn't think or write in terms of plot, or anything linear, to trust the fragment. Your generosity.

And a memory of you before I knew you, at the Arcane bookstore, sitting there at the front desk, in solitude, watching the shop, reading.

—

Alistair McCartney is the author of *The End of the World Book* and *The Disintegrations*.

Rose Michael – What you taught me

When I graduated, as a Doctor of Philosophy, I wondered what I'd learnt. Had the degree taught me how to write novels? Certainly it – and my supervisor, mostly my supervisor – had helped me write one. Perhaps (creative practice) research was what I'd learnt? But although I published the book, presented critical chapters as standalone papers and articles, my full thesis had an intimate audience of just three examiners. And you, my superior. Maybe the greatest insight my capstone qualification gave me was into the idiosyncratic bureaucracies of the university system. Of university's systems. But was that really the result of the PhD? The greatest gift, I realised in writing about that time, was our relationship. That unique experience, so generous and supportive, challenging and kind, was my introduction to – my induction into – how our writing and publishing industry works.

That's what I wrote then, 'industry', still seeing our world through my professional lens. Six years on I would say community. Now I see how, more than the way I write, what or how I research, your mentoring has shaped my own supervision. How I want to be, for students. With students. When I do my annual 'respectful research' training – learning that I shouldn't take presents, invite candidates to dinner, share personal stories – I think of you: cooking for me in your home, discussing insights into academia (particularly about being a woman in the academy). Sharing advice when I became pregnant and then parenting conversations when our Toms became teens. I wish I'd given you presents, Brenda. I changed universities and followed you across the country, driving across the Nullarbor and camping in the same halfway dustbowl, because of what I had (not) experienced previously. As if I knew what it would be like to be mentored by you.

My degree took me a long time to complete – a very long time. The absolute longest time permitted. It was probably thanks to you that I submitted in the end. You said you were retiring and would arrange another supervisor for me. I knew then it was time for me to finish up too. I wrote to you after that, apologising for the state of the work you had seen, reassuring you that I had developed my thinking, publishing proper outputs, justified your effort. That I was a legitimate academic, thanks to your patience and acceptance. And you wrote back in your calm, clear way: 'Oh good.' The supervisor kneels, you said, pins in mouth, taking in and letting out. Tucking and stitching the writer, I see now, as much as the writing.

—

Rose Michael wrote her second novel, *The Art of Navigation*, as a PhD with Brenda over ten years during which time she had two kids, renovated two houses, and changed jobs from publisher to lecturer.

Susan Midalia – In honour of Brenda Walker

Brenda was my colleague at UWA in the 1980s, when we both had a life of teaching and writing ahead of us, and again decades later, when I taught in her creative writing course. Brenda was widely admired by staff and students for her compassion, modesty, exquisite prose, and an enduring belief in the power of language and story to celebrate the complexities of people's lives. She was a gifted teacher, a generous colleague and, above all, a kind and gracious human being.

—

Susan Midalia is an author, mentor and editor, and Director of the Australian Short Story Festival, Perth chapter.

Carol Millner – With gratitude

The beginning of my friendship with Brenda coincided with a cluster of big life events: a divorce, a new job, and the transition to post-PhD life. On the one hand I was rehousing my family and reacquainting myself with the delights of Excel spreadsheets, and on the other I was accepting an Emerging Writers Program fellowship through the Katharine Susannah Prichard Writers' Centre. Only, I wasn't actually writing, and I couldn't see how I would. The PhD seemed to have sucked every last ounce of writerly brain out of me. I was floundering when a mutual friend suggested that I ask Brenda to be my mentor for the EWP fellowship.

So Brenda came into my life as a Beta reader, bringing her fine intelligence and decades of reading, writing, thinking and editing with her. Her slender figure and gentle smile belied an enormous energy. When my self-confidence was at an all-time low, she believed in me and in my writing and was a great encourager. 'No matter that you haven't published anything for a while,' she'd say. 'This is good. Keep going!'

Her comments and queries (always pencilled down the side of hard copy) sparked conversations about everything from crisp conclusions ('really necessary in the short form') to phrasing, tone, rhythm and word choice. Brenda was an exacting stylist, but she also encouraged me to focus more on the structure of my stories and essays, and to persevere with the pieces that demanded the most from me as a writer.

When the fellowship ended, I imagined that we would no longer meet but Brenda became one of the friends who helped me negotiate the transition from academia to afterwards. We met often in her beloved King's Park where we walked and talked or stopped for a coffee. We enjoyed long conversations about books, art, music, and writing …

I feel fortunate to have known Brenda and am so very grateful to have enjoyed even these three years of writerly friendship.

When we last spoke, Brenda had recently returned from a trip to Oslo with Alex, and she was quietly putting away the business of her mother's death. Afterwards she described a dream that she'd had and her pleasure at writing a fluent thirty thousand words towards her new novel while staying at her mother's house in New South Wales in the rain. After a challenging year, Brenda sounded eager to connect with friends in Melbourne over the break, before pressing on with her writing. We promised each other that we'd connect in the New Year.

Last Wednesday I opened Facebook on the bus to a joyful photo of Brenda at the top of my feed. I realised straight away that it must be one of the new portraits Alex had taken in Oslo and, as I hadn't seen her on Facebook for a while, I imagined that I was about to read an end of year round-up. When I read that Brenda was gone, I just sat. Even now, ten days on at the time of writing, it doesn't feel real. I can only imagine how hard it must be for Alex and Tom, Brenda's wider family and closest friends.

I hope it brings them some small degree of comfort to know how widely admired Brenda was for her writing and teaching, and how dearly she was loved by her friends.

May her memory be for a blessing.

—

Carol Millner writes poetry, short stories and essays and is General Manager of Sensorium Theatre.

Imbi Neeme – Memories of Brenda

Straight-backed and tall, Brenda moved – and thought – with precision and grace. As a teacher, she could be stern and sharp but also very funny in a quiet, considered way. I always loved the way she referred to her rockstar brother as 'Donald'.

From the moment I met her, I desperately wanted her to like me. Once, when I went to her home and she offered me a cup of tea, I was too embarrassed to admit I didn't like tea and ended up drinking two cups (black, with lots of sugar and lemon).

I also remember describing a group of people as 'plebs' to her. Brenda's disappointment in me was palpable and that moment taught me to be more careful with my words.

I was thrilled when she agreed to be my honours supervisor in 1991. I often joke that my dissertation in feminist performance theory has served me well in my career as an admin assistant. But the truth is, my year studying under Brenda profoundly shaped how I think about and engage with the world.

One day, I walked into her office in tears and despair. Everything I was reading and understanding only seemed to reveal how much more there was to read and understand. Brenda was gentle with me and reassured me that this was the mark of a good student, not a bad one. Thanks to her, I have never regarded my knowledge as absolute, and always strived to leave space to learn and grow.

Brenda was also the first person I knew who published a book. Until then, I had never considered it a possibility. Her gracious example showed me the way – even if it took me almost thirty years to follow it.

After that honours year, I left Perth to teach English in Japan. I always intended to return to UWA and complete my masters and PhD in the new creative writing program Brenda was developing, but the world swept me away. I like to imagine there is a version of me who did go back, who learned to love tea, and had long chats with Brenda in an office overlooking the New Fortune Theatre. But even without that, I've still felt her hand in all I've done and achieved.

I am so very grateful to have known her.

—

Imbi Neeme took her sweet time getting published, but finally managed to do it by winning the Penguin Literary Prize in 2019.

Kate Noske – Remembering kindness

My knowing Brenda was based in the circumstance of coming to UWA as a fresh graduate, hoping to make a career. She was the elegant, impressive, serene and intimidating woman I had only known through her writing, and Philip Mead, who offered me the casual position which brought me to WA, encouraged me to meet with her. I was terrified, waiting in the lobby of the Staff Club for Brenda. I was wearing my most 'proper academic' outfit, and trying to work out in advance what on earth I could say. Brenda walked through the doors and must have noticed immediately how nervous I was – the first thing she said to me was: 'Oh, you look right at home already!' It was exactly what I needed to hear. She then took me upstairs for a fancy lunch and made me feel very much her equal.

I will always be grateful to her for that welcome and induction into the faculty. Which isn't to say I didn't still find her intimidating! Her sheer intellectualism and grace of knowledge was always something to awe. Later, when she stepped down from her lectureship and I stepped into that role, she handed me over a single book of class readings, and I had the terrifying realisation that she was teaching all her units entirely from memory and her knowledge on the spot. She must have giggled to herself in that. I was horrified, and it was weeks of work to come even close to a basic competence, a level which she might have offered in her sleep.

I still strive to the level of adoration which her students seem universally to hold for her. Her wisdom and kindness as a teacher and a mentor, but even more so as a friend, will be long remembered. My love and condolences to you who feel her loss most keenly.

—

Catherine (Kate) Noske is an author and a lecturer in the English and Cultural Studies departments at UWA. She was the editor of *Westerly Magazine* from 2015 to 2023.

Kristina Olsson – With gratitude

Brenda Walker was a gifted writer and teacher, but to me her gifts were most apparent in her knack for friendship. We once lived and wrote together in a house in France; I will never forget her generosity as a reader, her gentle presence and fierce intellect. She taught me how to be calm in the throes of the writing process, how to harness the fierceness of the effort it demanded. How to laugh in its midst. I loved her for that.

—

Kristina Olsson is the author of *The China Garden*, *Shell*, and *Boy, Lost*, a family memoir.

Maria Papas – Brenda

When I think of Brenda, I think of her in her office at UWA. I think of the beautiful green beyond her window, the book titles on her shelves and the artwork on the wall above her desk. Mostly, I think of her with a teacup in her hand, a gentle and supportive listener. I am – in these memories – in the first, second … final years of my PhD, and she is offering encouragement or carefully imparting one or two clear pieces of advice intended to direct me forward, both in my writing and in life. We talk about motherhood. We talk about my research. We talk about the books that inspire us, and health, and music, and the whole time that I sit there, I am thinking how intelligent, how graceful, how deep the well of knowledge and generosity within her is. How lucky I am to be her student.

If I close my eyes, I will picture her even now in a crisp white shirt – linen probably – and a pair of pants or a skirt or jeans. I will hear her voice, and it will be kind and firm. She tells me that yes, I will finish this thesis, that quitting is not an option. She tells me that superannuation is important, especially for women. She says to open my heart, take care of myself. She says, sometimes the best we can do is not write. She teaches me to put the computer away, and journal instead, to observe the world and document what I see and hear and sense. And drafts later, she says my writing is good, and her opinion means the world to me.

From Brenda, I not only learn to hone my writing craft, I also learn the subtle empathy of a good mentor. Sometimes I see her in my own interactions with my senior school students. It's as though she is the standard by which I hope to teach by. I like to hold my teacup coming to class too. It's not china like hers, but rather one of those thermal mugs with a fitted lid. Still, it signals to me to impart the same kindness she once gave so freely; it signals to listen.

I am beyond devasted to hear of her passing. I feel our world has lost one of its most humble and generous souls, and I will miss her.

Much love,
Maria

—

Maria Papas is both a writer and an English teacher. Her first novel, *Skimming Stones*, written as the creative component of a PhD, won the 2020 City of Fremantle Hungerford Award, and has since been published with Fremantle Press.

Marcella Polain – The surface of the river

My memory is that I first met Brenda in 1991 at the home of a new (now dear) writer-friend who, like me, had recently left a marriage. Brenda had just won the Hungerford; my new friend mentioned this, and I remember the shy pleasure on Brenda's face, her smile, the small bow of her head as I congratulated her. I was so new to the writing scene that, while I gleaned this was an important achievement, I didn't actually know what the Hungerford was. It might even have been that *Crush* had just been released or was about to be – either way, I think Brenda was the first writer I had ever met who had won a significant prize or had a book-length publication. Of course, I was in awe.

She was born only a year before me, but I didn't know that then. Her intonation, her eloquence, her manners, carriage, confidence. Her success. The seeming-ease with which she moved through the world. Immediately, I saw she came from a place I knew little of. A place at the centre of things. Of certainty, belonging, financial security. It was clear she was on her way. I felt a little like I was sitting at the kitchen table with the queen. We drank tea. I was self-conscious, like a kid, like the migrant I am, an impostor. But I enjoyed witnessing the obvious connection between my new friend and Brenda; they had known one another for years, were so comfortable in one other's company.

The three of us had small children; we talked about our lives. She asked about my writing. There wasn't much to say. I had just returned to it after a decade-long hiatus, had published nothing. Then I listened and watched the two of them chat, their referring to ideas and theorists I had never heard of. So this, I thought to myself, is the world of serious writers.

My education felt suddenly inadequate and outmoded, my passion for William Faulkner or Antonin Artaud useless in the fervour of Australian women's writing of the time. These two writers were informed by Feminist Literature, particularly the French Feminists; they knew and practised women's experimental fiction. They were highly theorised, and spoke fiercely, urgently from these theories to the core concerns of our lives. It felt alien and thrilling.

We were so young, still in our early thirties. We were all lithe, but I remember being struck by the way Brenda moved with deliberate grace. I wanted to be like her and knew that was impossible.

Over the ensuing years, my new friend would once or twice mention Brenda's sorrows. Stupidly, I was surprised. Yes, everyone has sorrows – but somehow I didn't think that would ever include Brenda. So well did she protect her privacy, her dignity.

When I taught creative writing at the University of Western Australia, and then began my doctoral studies there, Brenda and I saw a little of one another. She was curious about my research and, one afternoon, we sat by the Swan River and drank tea again, and she asked me about it, about my family history and how I was using it for my novel. I was nervous. She was so accomplished.

Where did your family come from? she asked.

I told her. She had been to Istanbul, she said – at that time, I hadn't – and she described it for me, at length. I remember gazing at the surface of the river, mesmerised, as I listened and imagined.

Then, I said: And did you go to Constantinople? I turned to her. She seemed to be looking at the ground, paused. She frowned just a little. I waited.

Well, yes, she replied. As I said …

Oh, of course, yes, I said, turning away to the river again, all its glittering light. We moved on to another topic.

I have thought of that moment many times. I'd like to think that I knew that Constantinople had been renamed and had simply forgotten – but I don't know whether that's true. What I do know is that in my family, in the world of my research and in the Western Armenian Diaspora, Constantinople still exists. In my mind, the two were different places, which of course they are.

For years I felt humiliated by that memory. I'd betrayed something about very private about myself, some limitation, some ignorance, confusion. Or some version of reality that marked me. Now, what I remember most about that moment is this: she didn't laugh at or correct or interrogate or admonish me. With her usual grace, she allowed me to preserve my dignity.

I think that was the last lengthy face-to-face conversation we had.

I can't remember if I went to the launch of *Crush*. It's unlikely – my children were small, my copy isn't signed. None of my copies of her books are signed. I always thought there was time – that once I'd retired, I'd remedy things like that. If only we could know what's ahead of us. We might be funnier, braver – turn faux pas into jokes, care less about appearing foolish, explain ourselves a bit better, ask a writer we admire to please sign.

If she were here, I would tell her that one of the most important breakthroughs in my writing practice was initiated by her asking me to write two essays for *The Writer's Reader*. Those pieces were the first time I wrote what we then called fictocriticism, and I can still feel the all-consuming demand and thrill of it. Terrified, I sent the pieces to her. Her reply was swift, affirming. I still see the computer screen in front of me, the view from the window I turned to gaze through. Still feel my heart leap at her reassurance that I can really do this writing-thing.

In the blurb which she kindly wrote for my first novel, despite us not having contact for years, she mentions 'the dimensions of suffering and love'. These two: the palm and the back of the same hand which, together, make writing possible.

For days, I've been trying to find a way to finish this reflection with the appropriate elegance. Elegance was strong in Brenda. It's not so in me. I haven't found a way and now there's no more time. I can only offer her my thanks.

—

Marcella Polain is a poet, novelist, essayist and Senior Lecturer in Creative and Professional Writing at Edith Cowan University, Boorloo (Perth).

Andrew Relph – Inspiration

There are gifts we are given which keep on rewarding us. Alive, she helped us write so that we could hear what it was we were thinking and feeling. Now in the sad aftermath of her death we are called to 'give sorrow words'. This is a challenge, yet we brave ones, like Brenda, know we must make an attempt. Words will help us in the sad and often lonely days of staying when those we love have left.

I always thought Brenda had an other-worldly presence. So it is not surprising that I see her still as one of the Graces – sister goddesses of beauty, grace and charm.

Yet really she was another kind of goddess she was a Muse. A Muse to many. I often referred to Brenda as: *my friend and writing teacher*. How many hundreds of people did? Scrutiny can be intimidating or encouraging. Meetings with Brenda left me encouraged.

Brenda had the rare gift to inspire creativity.

It was somehow related to her quirky breath control. She would read a novice's work with astonishing speed. Often there would be a sharp in-breath when something touched her. Later when considering how to approach what it was she was going to say about the writing there would be a vividly conscious out-breath often accompanied by a dreamy gaze at something in the distance.

She was taking you with her while deeply considering what it was you were saying. Hardly anyone reads another person with such concentrated attention on what is there. It takes unusual generosity.

The ensuing conversation about the work would take you to a place where you had been all along but this time with the consciousness of words.

Brenda could inspire you to write what it was you were thinking and feeling, to say what it was you wanted to say. Her informing clarity always seemed to leave space for your unique voice to emerge and be heard.

Like all good conversations with the spaciousness for things to unfold, this one is left incomplete.

I'm full of gratefulness for Brenda and the limitless effect she had on me. That will continue.

—

Andrew Relph is a clinical psychologist and psychotherapist, and the author of the memoir *Not Drowing, Reading*.

Richard Rossiter – Hungerford judges

I didn't know Brenda especially well, but we caught up not so long ago during the Hungerford judging. We shared some of life's more challenging experiences and I was struck by her quiet wisdom, her understated manner, her perceptiveness. Her generosity.

On reading some of the online comments, I made a note of a quote from *Reading by Moonlight* that seemed particularly apposite:

> *We each have one life, one share of action and vision and money; a single life for all our speech and thought, our decent gestures and the decisions that might undo us, our welcome or unwanted love, our parties that may or may not come off. One life to satisfy our vast and human sense of voyaging. With the right books we find out what imaginary strangers have done with their share of this amazing thing, life.*

Brenda was a highly accomplished writer and academic whose work spanned generations, locations, genres. Her support for other writers is widely acknowledged.

—

Richard Rossiter is a writer, editor and occasional mentor and judge of writing competitions. He is Honorary Associate Professor at Edith Cowan University.

Bruce Russell – One who gladly led

Brenda Walker arrived in my life at a time when I could no longer contain the urge to write a full-length work of fiction. There she was, a true academic with all the right credentials – and a novelist to boot.

She was also very kind to me, my first mentor. She and Dennis Haskell gave me the nod for the masters program, an unlikely candidate for sure. An Economics degree? When I told her about my work she smiled and said, 'Ah, a real job.' She read my early stories, looked at my meagre bag of prizes and judged me to have 'paid my dues' as a writer. And then she agreed to take me on. We wrote *Jacob's Air* together – I wrote it and she guided me every step of the way, right down to telling me how unlikely it was that my main character, Delmarie, would make a special trip to buy make-up. When I entered it in the Hungerford she was doubtful that it was ready; but then, I have always been in a hurry. When it won, she launched the book, a night I will never forget.

I came away from all that thinking that I was one of her favourites, me and Alice Nelson. That probably sounds ridiculous now and anyhow, what does it matter? But as Georgia Richter has said elsewhere,[1] she came into my life at a very delicate moment and profoundly influenced its direction. Whenever I ran into

1 'Vale Brenda Walker (1957 to 2024)', fremantlepress.com.au/2024/12/13/vale-brenda-walker-1957-to-2024, 13 December 2024.

her over the years, she would gently prod me to keep writing. And so I did. She marked my PhD and had lots to say about the misogynous main character in the novel that was part of it. Along with Wendy Jenkins, she is right up there in my memory of writing elders.

I know how much she gave to the writing world, much more than a few obituaries can contain. I will miss her enormously.

—

Bruce Russell's first novel, *Jacob's Air*, won the TAG Hungerford Award in 1995, and was published by FACP in 1996. He has since published five more novels and three commissioned biographies.

Tracy Ryan – From scratch

So much went into it,
that moment among many,

really an interregnum,
there in your townhouse,

both of us temporarily
alone, rebuilding and yet

our children with instant
rapport happy to play

while you sought a way to meet
needs others called *difficult*

back when almost nobody
knew what *vegan* meant:

Apples occurred to me –
simplest is best, you said, laid out

a mountain we duly
processed along with the rest

of what was taxing us,
exactly the same

as your coming to see me
years before when I was broken,

talking me through with care
from the beginning / like finding a rhythm

till that heap was reduced
and stewed, and the kitchen warm

with the least hint of sweetness
and cinnamon, for a shared feast.

—

Tracy Ryan is a Western Australian writer whose most recent book is *The Queen's Apprenticeship* (Transit Lounge, 2023).

Bron Sibree – On the loss of Brenda Walker

How to deal with the senseless loss of Brenda Walker? When one of Brenda's dearest friends phoned me with news of her death, I struggled to believe it. Surely someone somewhere had made a terrible error? Even now, knowing the awful fact of it, it seems akin to some terrible celestial mistake that has left me and countless others reeling and bereft. So my heartfelt condolences to her husband, her son and her brothers. Like all those who knew her, to not hear her wise, insightful words again, her voice, or read her beautiful books, let alone to not have the benefit of her generosity and beautiful spirit is an indelible sadness. Being the extraordinarily gifted writer she was, she leaves Australia with an esteemed literary legacy but it is the memory of her generous kind spirit that will live on in my heart and mind. Her untimely senseless death is a reminder to treasure and be kind to all those around us.

—

Bron Sibree is a freelance journalist who's written for various publications in Australia and Asia for more than twenty years.

Gerry Turcotte – Two poems for Brenda Walker

Varuna diary

for Brenda Walker

Day one:
Potter, organise your files
Walk into town
Turn computer one

Day two:
Fiddle with the fonts
Widen margins
Turn computer off

Day three:
Have major breakthrough
Restructure heavily
Forget to save

Day four:
Holy of holies
Run screaming with excitement
The manuscript's complete!

Day five:

Come to your senses
        The book is crap
And 20,000 words too short

Day six:

Recover from hangover
        Vow to give up smoking
Never touch another drop

Day seven:

Hate fellow writers
        They are better than you
They're almost finished

Day eight:

The pieces fit
        The manuscript is done
No one believes you

Day nine:

Wonder what day it is
        Word count is an hourly routine
Your novel's a haiku

Day ten:

Insist the book is finished
        Brenda smiles politely

A few more days to go

Day eleven:
Wrap everything up
          Try to like yourself
You've made a good start

Day twelve:
Enrol in plumbing course
          Get gold licence
Learn a new language

❧

Bookshelf in the Sewing Room: Varuna

Reading by moonlight
    at the wing of night

Poe's cat
    crosses one more river
        in the feral city

Thérèse Raquin and Lewis Carroll
    brush shoulders
        with the honorary consul

who is waiting for Godot
    in the land that time forgot

but all I see now
    are the empty spaces
        where your unwritten works should be

—

Gerry Turcotte is President of St Mark's College in Vancouver, Canada. His first novel, *Flying in Silence*, which was shortlisted for *The Age* Book of the Year, was written during a Varuna residency under Brenda Walker's guidance.

Wendy Waring – Remembering Brenda

I'd met you at conferences, and admired your scholarship and your fiction, of course, but our story starts with your tap on the doorjamb of my new office at UWA. You'd come to tell me about the peahen and its new and many chicks. Later, I remember sitting up late with you at my place in Sydney, dissecting the world. Such a delightfully wicked sense of humour you had, a surprising partner to your elegance. And your writerly generosity was extraordinary. You published my very first fiction, in *Westerly*, and you made me feel like it was unique. When life sailed me abroad, I failed to stay properly in touch, thinking we'd soon enjoy a proper face-to-face chinwag. Foolish human. Now you are gone. In my memory, you stand ever tall, a smile in the doorway, come to share joy.

—

Born in Canada, buoyed up by Oz, **Wendy Waring** is a writer, translator, editor and lecturer.

David Whish-Wilson & Belinda Rowe – How to be a writer in the world

I wasn't a close friend of Brenda's. Our relationship was always defined by her generous support for me as a writer, and I have always thought of her as a wise and caring mentor. I had read her work without meeting her when I first returned from Japan to live here, in the mid-90s. It was my wife, Belinda Rowe, one of Brenda's students at UWA, who gave me first impressions of her as a lecturer, and as a person. Belinda had left school aged fifteen, and for her to be in the presence of two women, both Brenda and her colleague Gail Jones, so sharply intelligent and charismatic, so caring of their subject and committed to how it might be communicated to novice writers, made a deep impression upon her. Brenda then examined her honours thesis, reinforcing Belinda's earlier impression of Brenda as generous and supportive, which is also how I came to meet Brenda, when she examined my doctoral thesis. When the novel that formed the creative element of that doctoral thesis, *The Summons*, went on to be published, it was Brenda's endorsement that adorned the cover. The publication also led to our first meeting. I was of course a little overawed and a little shocked to be treated as an equal – somebody Brenda was keen to chat with about books and writing. I can't remember where that meeting took place, but I'll never forget her words. At a certain point she said to me, 'Dave, you're a writer's writer.' Never good at receiving compliments, I probably mumbled, 'Thanks, I appreciate it.' It was then that her posture and voice changed, and she leaned closer. 'It's not a good thing. Other writers can see what you're trying to do, but that doesn't mean that readers will. Do you understand?'

I understood, and it's something I think about, a lot, when I'm working, all these years later. I've wondered, too, at her change in tone, her leaning forward, the only moment in many subsequent meetings where such honesty and forthrightness had been required to impress upon me an important truth. Since that first meeting, I've generally met Brenda when she's contacted me about a new release, to offer her support, or once or twice to try and convince me to shift universities, or the numerous times when I've walked out onto a stage at a writer's festival, to see her in the audience, there again purely to show support. Invariably we caught up afterward for a coffee, generally talking about our sons, me often thanking her for having heard on the grapevine that she'd championed my work to someone – a publisher, an agent, a reviewer, an academic, for no reason except natural generosity, something expressed in deeds as much as words.

I consider myself a lucky writer, for having had terrific early mentors in Bruce Pascoe, Deborah Robertson, Joan London and Brenda Walker. What each have in common, apart from the example of their writing and their commitment to the craft, is something exemplified in Brenda's generosity toward me as a younger writer – how she modelled for me (someone who came to writing from left-field, not knowing any other writers, or anything about the culture and business of writing) how a writer might move through the world – not with ego, or competitiveness, or envy, but with a kind heart and a love of the craft, helping others wherever possible. That Brenda did this for so many writers is a wonderful legacy, on top of her many achievements as a writer of beautiful prose. I'll always be grateful for the gift of her support, advice and encouragement.

—

David Whish-Wilson is a Fremantle-based writer of fiction and non-fiction.

Belinda Rowe is a flash-fiction writer and teacher.

Bob White – Brenda Walker

The last time I saw Brenda was fleetingly at the morning Windsor Cinema screening of an art movie on either Van Gogh's sunflowers or Monet's garden, I can't remember which. Either way, it is a beautiful, intertwined memory to treasure, a relaxing occasion garlanded with flowers and the radiance of art. A wonderful colleague and caring teacher and supervisor, Brenda made significant contributions to UWA. She helped to initiate and develop the distinguished Creative Writing program, was an inspiring presence in the Women in Leadership project, and in other unobtrusive and thoughtful ways. In both writing and conversation she had a virtuoso ability to say a multitude of things in succinct, multi-layered ellipses. Her unique way of looking at the world and representing it in her novels was a gift, sharply observant and deeply humane. Wise, witty and kind, Brenda's words leave many traces of her distinctive voice for us to read and remember her by.

—

Bob White has been Winthrop Professor of English and head of the English Department at UWA. His latest book is *Shakespeare Against War* (Edinburgh University Press, 2024).

Chris Wortham – Brenda Walker

Brenda had many gifts, but the best if them all was herself. She was immensely intelligent and she was also infinitely kind. A smile from Brenda would make one's day. Though Brenda and I tended to work in diverse areas, as a somewhat older colleague I particularly came to value her gift for supervising postgrads to successful conclusion. As the department of English grew and diversified, Brenda became a canny and benign guiding force for many. We all remember her as someone whose judgement we valued and whose friendship we treasured. Brenda will be greatly missed by us all.

—

Chris Wortham has worked since 1977 both at UWA and at the University of Notre Dame. He is now an Emeritus Professor at UWA.

Jacqueline Wright – All it took was an hour

I met Brenda once, for an hour, and she changed my life around. I'd been successful getting offers for two creative arts PhDs, one with UWA, the other with Curtin. One with a stipend, the other without. I wasn't sure I should attempt either (it had been a long time between uni degrees for me). I was pregnant, lived 3,000Ks away and had zero confidence I could take on a post-graduate degree. Brenda, who'd read a rough first(ish) draft of my novel, assured me I could. I don't remember her exact words, just her blaze of belief in me that set my path as a writer. Taking Brenda's advice, I enrolled in the institution that had offered me a stipend, so I didn't get to work with her. But her confidence in what I was writing helped enormously to bolster the perseverance it takes for a debut novelist to achieve publication. *Red Dirt Talking* thanks you, Brenda, and so do I.

—

Jacqueline Wright has a creative arts doctorate from Curtin University, where she wrote her first novel. It went on to win the TAG Hungerford Award in 2010 and was longlisted for the Miles Franklin Literary Award.

Will Yeoman – Remembering Brenda Walker

Brenda Walker's loss will be keenly felt not just by her family and friends but by the Australian literary community. Her novels, stories and the memoir *Reading by Moonlight: How Books Saved a Life* garnered significant popular and critical acclaim; but her sublime writing was matched by her gifts as a mentor. I recall with fondness the sporadic but intense and wide-ranging discussions we enjoyed over the years, especially during my time as literary Editor at *The West Australian*. Another light in the literary firmament has just been extinguished and our ways are now less certain.

—

Will Yeoman is the Chief Executive Officer of Writing WA.

This piece first appeared in writingwa.org/news/remembering-brenda-walker, 12 December 2024.

Anne-Louise Willoughby – In her words

My need to hear Brenda's voice is pressing, and our email correspondence during my PhD offers up solace. I read and hear her generous supervisor voice transitioning over the years of messages to that of friend; the generosity coupled with the elegance of her word choices brings her breathy speaking voice to my inner ear and straight to my heart.

I had a moment with Brenda before I started the process of moving from short-form writing to long form, from two thousand words to one hundred and twenty thousand. I sat in front of her in her UWA office, poised with pen and paper; as a career journalist I was ready for the gold. I had made a special appointment to interview my Captain – what strategy, what preparation can I do to make this jump?

The window behind Brenda with its view to the lawns and trees of the Arts Building precinct created a spill of light over her shoulders. In a kind of beatific pose, she held her two hands softly in her lap, she paused and leaned back in her chair. I leaned forward in mine waiting for the wisdom. 'Just start,' she said, and smiled. 'You have no idea what is sitting in your subconscious, but it is there and you will find it. Just start.'

Many times I returned to that chair for supervision meetings, for advice, or just to say hello when PhD-itis had taken hold and progress seemed impossible. It is a fact that I would not have this second career as a biographer with a successful book if not for Brenda. Her faith in my ability, when my own was wanting, spurred me on. Her generosity is something I keep returning to, her willingness to gift her knowledge with grace and encouragement so profound that sometimes I floated when I left her room, renewed.

In the years that a PhD takes, and the hundreds of hours exchanged in work and thought, a friendship was cemented. We shared common ground as women born in the late 1950s, as wives, as single mothers, remarried women, as writers, as daughters of formidable and brilliant mothers in their nineties, and, wonderfully, as young women in the unique pub music scene of the seventies with brothers in bands. It wasn't until I had begun postgrad work that I learned that Brenda had attended my husband's funeral. She was my teacher, my daughter's teacher, and my son's. I loved that she had come. He had died in early 2008 two months after I completed my undergraduate degree, when my relationship with Brenda was in its embryonic phase. My return to honours with her in 2010 was my attempt to regain some kind of control after losing him and it was during this period of writing memoir that our deeper connection grew as I wrote around the cataclysmic event. He believed in me as a writer, he was my champion. Then Brenda took the baton from him and carried me forward. In my darkest hours she was there with words of comfort, not couched in sympathy – though of course it was present – but gilded with fortitude that she believed I possessed. For years, Brenda's words, wrapped in an unequivocal belief in my capabilities, sustained me. The work was an ever-expanding exploration of that subconscious well of thoughts, beliefs, ideas; of the things we know we don't know but are willing to search for – and I had Brenda as my guide. I recall likening her role to Virgil's, walking alongside Dante as he descended into Purgatory: she would see me safely out.

Our shared experience as only daughters, sisters of two creative brothers, was filled with understanding of the subtleties that this rank holds. Her electronic letters to me encouraged me as I watched *my* Shirley, while she spent the final years with hers, her grace ever present, and her way of describing a scene an artful thing that regularly left me feeling bathed in greatness:

> *Dear Anne-Louise,*
>
> *I haven't opened the computer for a few days and I got your text this morning. I arrived at my mother's house last night after a little time in Sydney with my friend Anita. Sydney was spectacular – I've included a photo. All the books I have on a list to order were cover-uppermost in the Potts Point bookshop. I could watch the view from this window forever – a minute after this picture was taken the buildings were sheeted in rose coloured light.*
>
> *Now I'm with Granny – see photo. Jane, the neighbour brought these roses and the vase was bought by my grandfather as a gift for my great-grandmother – from his first pay cheque. The house is full of things like this.*

Granny is surprisingly well and very independent, she covers up her frailty. She came close to hospitalization and worse the week before last, with pneumonia. Richard has been watching her during the night. Now I'm here for a fortnight. I'll be back in October for another stretch. I think she's recovering but when very elderly people decline it's sudden and dangerous.

I have several nests here. A cedar table to write on, with a view down a valley to the sea. A deep cosy chair, very much an old-person nest, to watch TV with Granny. The studio with the big piano which I'm trying to adjust to – the music seems so far away and the action is quite stiff. Our childhood piano is lighter but I am determined to work with the monster!

So you see, I can't come to lunch although a Matilda Bay lunch with a view over the water would be very good.

Stay warm and dry!

xxxBrenda.

Nests, eyries, like her Kings Park home, demonstrated her eye for beauty and the arrangement of things that fed this artist. Visitors could read her through her arrangements. Her piano and playing music were central to her equilibrium. The piano, bought for its petiteness and suitability for apartment living, was also chosen for its superlative machining and she honoured that with her discipline in taking lessons, and the practice that was not a chore. This discipline is something I am still trying to emulate, her rigour of being at her desk each morning even if for just one very good sentence.

> *Today I have done my 250 words just on dawn with the rain coming down and a blow heater grinding away at ankle height. I need to do another 250 later. My little story is growing. The style is still there. I've spent the past two years rushing about and I've come to the conclusion that nothing can be achieved in the midst of errands. Cooking is different, cooking feeds the soul. (Yesterday my piano teacher said hesitantly at the end of our lesson: Do you believe it touches your soul? And I said yes, of course it does. Even scales touch the soul.)*

A text from Brenda was never just a message.

> *Thank you so much for visiting today. I do think everything around us is so much more vibrant now. We really had burdensome lives when you began that PhD. The book has done so well and you are so much happier*

and so am I in my little house in the sky. With Chopin. I will play you the Suffocation Prelude any time. You can look it up on YouTube! My nocturne is 72. Listen to it sometime it is the most beautiful thing. XxxB

On the possibility of my book being adapted for film Brenda wrote but, as she regularly did, she expanded my enquiry into something wider. She taught me the power and place of context.

What I love about publishing a book is that it's wise to keep expectations to a minimum but just sometimes a book spools on and on for years, delivering readers' messages and the occasional jolt of film options and teaching interest. Film writing is difficult – it must be simplified but not simple. You'll get there. I've been reading a book by Alan Rusbridger called Play it Again. *He was the editor of the* Guardian *(UK) and he decided, at a time of extraordinary global political disruption, to take a year to learn a very difficult Chopin piece. The objective is to play it not well but credibly. He quotes Jung – and I think you will like this: 'A human being would certainly not grow to be 70 or 80 years old if this longevity had no meaning for the species to which he belongs. […] Moneymaking, social existence, family and posterity are nothing but plain nature – not culture. Culture lies beyond the purpose of nature. Could by any chance culture be the meaning and purpose of the second half of life?'*

We enjoyed going out to lunch and would take turns in choosing the restaurant. At the end of my PhD in 2021, after the publication of the book that resulted because I followed her advice to 'just start', it was time to celebrate:

Dear Anne Louise,

I think it would be nice to meet for lunch to celebrate so many years of guidance on my part and, at graduation, fulfillment on yours. Your pact with your husband has come to fruition. Your new life as a writer now has a sound foundation which will sustain you through familial complexities. One day you will be an old woman with a shelf of your own books – the objective we all aim for.

The poet Kate Llewellyn once wrote that art has married her with a blue ring and there are no divorces ever. I love this, it is a different kind of marriage.

I'm available on Thursday at 12.30 if you would like to eat at the [Uni] Club, although of course there are other places.

all the best,

Brenda.

I replied that that would suit, and how affirming I found the Llewellyn quote. I could see Brenda arriving for our lunch in Isabel Marant silk and a pair of ballerina flats. Her head would be slightly tilted and we'd peck on the cheek and I'd catch a glimpse of an antique ring or brooch artfully worn and elegantly understated – like her prose. She responded:

> *The Llewellyn quote is very special. It isn't just a matter of divorce, it's loss of the kind you've suffered. Art/writing isn't as funny or warming as a sweet husband like Alex or Tim, but it is rich and engaging and euphoric and despairing and sustaining into old age (Peter [Straus] and I are negotiating a contract now at 64 and this will not be my last book). And the ring the artist wears is blue, because making art is, at heart, sad – it is done in defiance of death, which means a tacit acknowledgement of death.*
>
> *12.30. Club! Dress code: dressy. Oh, very dressy.*
>
> *xB*

—

Anne-Louise Willoughby is a biographer and author of *Nora Heysen: a portrait*, written as the creative component of her PhD at UWA under Brenda Walker's supervision, and published by Fremantle Press in 2019.

Vale Brenda Walker

(18.7.1957–10.12.2024)

www.ingramcontent.com/pod-product-compliance
Lightning Source LLC
Chambersburg PA
CBHW040227170726
48295CB00014B/829

* 9 7 8 1 7 6 0 9 9 6 5 7 4 *